WITHDRAWN

PRELIMINARY EXCAVATION REPORTS:

Sardis, Paphos, Caesarea Maritima, Shiqmim, ᶜAin Ghazal

THE ANNUAL OF
THE AMERICAN SCHOOLS OF ORIENTAL RESEARCH

Volume 51

Edited By

William G. Dever

PRELIMINARY EXCAVATION REPORTS:

Sardis, Paphos, Caesarea Maritima, Shiqmim, ᶜAin Ghazal

Edited by

William G. Dever

American Schools of Oriental Research

PRELIMINARY EXCAVATION REPORTS
SARDIS, PAPHOS, CAESAREA MARITIMA, SHIQMIM, AIN GHAZAL

Edited by
William G. Dever

© 1994
American Schools of Oriental Research

Library of Congress Cataloging in Publication Data
Preliminary excavation reports : Sardis, Paphos, Caesarea Maritima,
Shiqmim, Ain Ghazal / edited by William G. Dever.
    p.   cm. — (The Annual of the American Schools of Oriental
Research ; v. 51)
    ISBN 1-55540-926-1 (cloth)
    1. Excavations (Archaeology) Middle East. 2. Middle East—
Antiquities. I. Dever, William G. II. Series.
DS101.A45 vol. 51
[DS56]
939'.4—dc20   93-40735
                                                     CIP

Printed in the United States of America
on acid-free paper

Contents

The Sardis Campaigns of 1988 and 1989

CRAWFORD H. GREENEWALT, JR.
Department of Classics
University of California
Berkeley, CA 94720

CHRISTOPHER RATTÉ
Department of Classics
Florida State University
Tallahassee, FL 32306

MARCUS L. RAUTMAN
Department of Art History and Archaeology
University of Missouri
Columbia, MO 65211

Excavation focused on two regions of the city site. In sectors MMS, MMS/N, and MMS/S, a Late Roman stratum produced more of two residential units (with artifacts that included a deacon's seal), a colonnaded street, and a colonnaded avenue, while an Archaic stratum produced more of Colossal Lydian Structure and the destruction deposit that may be associated with the Persian capture of Sardis in 546–542 B.C.E.; the latter contained a soldier's (?) skeleton. In sector ByzFort, Archaic strata yielded the marble stylobate of a small colonnaded building of the sixth century B.C.E. and deposits of the seventh century B.C.E. Graves were excavated in 1989 by the Expedition (Hellenistic [?] chamber tomb in the city cemetery) and by the Archaeological Museum in Manisa (ten sarcophagus burials of the fifth-to-second centuries B.C.E. in the city cemetery, one sarcophagus burial and one tumulus tomb of the sixth century B.C.E. at Bin Tepe; the last yielded remains of a funeral cart or chariot). In addition to excavation, conservation, recording, study, and communication projects were components of both field season programs.

The results of excavation and closely related activities at Sardis in 1988 and 1989 are the subject of this report.[1] The objectives, in addition to excavation, included conservation, recording, study, and communication projects, notably the following: balloon photography of the city site; graphic recording of the Artemis Temple; and studies of Greek and Latin inscriptions recovered in previous seasons; Lydian masonry at Sardis and Bin Tepe (see Ratté 1989); Iron Age stratification and pottery from sector HoB; Iron Age and Archaic stratification and pottery from sector PC; Hellenistic pottery; Later Roman pottery from two wells at sector MMS (see Rautman 1990; this article, below); ancient plant remains and modern comparanda. Display proposals were also prepared for the Archaeological and Ethnographical Museum in Manisa.[2] The current report is based on reports written in the field by Expedition staff members; copies of those reports are filed in the Sardis Expedition Office at Harvard University.

Excavation concentrated on the two regions of the city site that have been the focus of excavation in recent seasons: sectors MMS, MMS/N, and MMS/S, located below and to the northwest of the Acropolis (fig. 1A), and sector ByzFort, a low spur on the north flank of the Acropolis (fig. 1B). In addition, a chamber tomb in the city cemetery west of the Pactolus stream was excavated (fig. 1C). The priority since 1977 has been to clarify urban topography and monuments of the Lydian and early Persian periods in the seventh and sixth centuries B.C.E.

C.H.G.

SECTORS MMS, MMS/N, AND MMS/S

Sector MMS, with its north and south adjunct sectors MMS/N and MMS/S, is centered on the low hill at the end of a northwest spur of the Acropolis

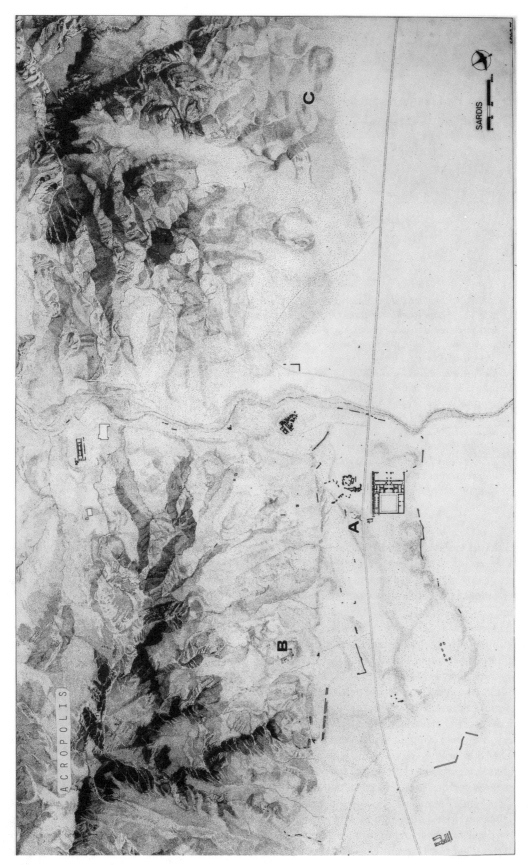

Fig. 1. Sardis, visual relief map of site and immediate environs, with south at top. A = sector MMS; B = sector ByzFort; C = Haci Oğlan site in city cemetery.

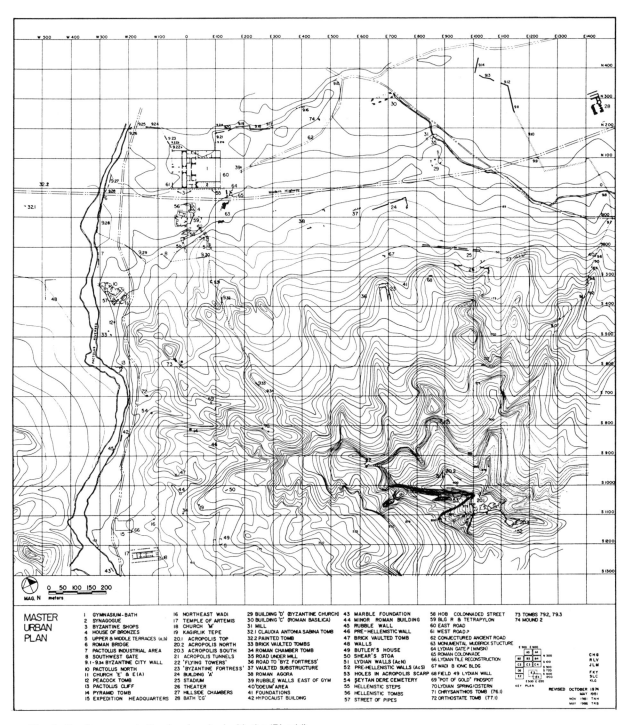

Fig. 2. Sardis, general site plan (marked with the 'B' grid).

near the modern Ankara-Izmir highway (figs. 1A; 2, nos. 63, 65). Excavations since 1977 have demonstrated that the hill is formed by the debris of a monumental building of the late seventh and sixth centuries B.C.E., known as Colossal Lydian Structure. Recent field seasons have explored this and other features of Archaic Lydian date, as well as levels of Late Roman times, when the locale was built over by a number of residential structures (Greenewalt 1990: 1–28 and references).

Sectors MMS, MMS/N, and MMS/S, Roman Levels

Over the last ten years excavations in the MMS sectors have revealed a densely built quarter of the Late Roman period. Among the remains are several elegant townhouses that opened onto broad colonnaded streets (fig. 3). Work in 1988 and 1989 continued to clarify the form and history of this neighborhood of western Sardis, from its initial development by the early fifth century through its abandonment in the late sixth and early seventh centuries C.E.

MMS/N.   Sector MMS/N lies immediately north of the modern highway opposite the hill of MMS. Located near the southeast corner of the Roman Bath-Gymnasium and Synagogue complexes, the sector includes monumental architecture of both Lydian and Roman times, as well as fragmentary remains of intervening periods. Previous work in the area identified a broad plaza-like intersection of two Roman streets with part of a colonnaded ambulatory extending along its south side (Greenewalt, Sterud, and Belknap 1982: 15–21; Greenewalt *et al.* 1983: 10–15). Excavation in 1989 concentrated on exposing more of that portico and its mosaic floors.

The major feature of the south ambulatory is the monumental colonnade that defines the south side of the marble-flagged expanse. The line of that colonnade extends the full 24 m width of excavation (E. 127–151 on the 'B' grid), and is attested by a continuous stylobate, several column bases, and fragments of column shafts. As noted in earlier years, the stylobate does not continue the orientation of the colonnade exposed in front of the Byzantine Shops further west (which is oriented on the 'B' grid) but angles toward the northeast. Even within Sector MMS/N the construction of the colonnade consists of two distinct sections. The western part presents four large 0.80 m Attic Ionic column bases set at 2.40 m interaxial intervals. The less well preserved eastern section preserves traces of two smaller pedestal bases, for which an interval of 2.62 m over a distance of 13.1 m may be suggested.[3] Both sections of the colonnade share the same stylobate of irregularly set marble blocks, which step gradually upward from west to east. At a later date some of the bases were incorporated into the rising stylobate. Presumably both sections supported a portico that covered the mosaic-paved sidewalk to the south.

About 6 to 8 m behind the monumental west colonnade stands its back wall, constructed of brick and fieldstone and surviving to a height of over 2 m (fig. 4). This feature more closely follows the 'B' grid and so lies askew of the axis of the north colonnade. Its east end is marked by a strongly projecting pier built of large marble blocks (at E. 138 on the 'B' grid). To the west the wall ends in an ashlar terminus, beyond which extends a monumental threshold of two or more steps to a width of at least 2.5 m. The structure, of which this wall formed the north facade, lies beneath the present roadway.

The sidewalk area between the western colonnade and its back wall was covered with two superimposed mosaic floors. Previous excavation suggested an early fifth century C.E. date for the lower surface, which presents a central zone of interlocked squares surrounded by a triple guilloche and ivy rinceau border. A less well preserved mosaic with scale pattern was installed 0.35 m higher, apparently in the later sixth century C.E. (Greenewalt, Sterud, and Belknap 1982: 17). While details of phasing still await confirmation, the lower mosaic seems to have been contemporary with or slightly later than the colonnade and the back wall. A new drain ran northward under the upper mosaic, which may have been installed around the time the colonnade stylobate was raised. The threshold in the south wall apparently was installed or relocated atop this later surface.

The eastern section of the MMS/N colonnade rested on smaller 0.60 m pedestal bases, of which two were identified by earlier excavation. The area was thoroughly stripped in late antiquity, and few traces of the standing order still survive. Approximately 6 to 7 m behind those columns stood a second colonnade, which was exposed in 1989 to a length of 9.5 m. This feature is attested by four large column bases that extend to the northeast from the projecting ashlar pier of the back wall, converging slightly toward the front colonnade to the east. Set against the projecting pier, the westernmost element of the inner colonnade consisted of an inscribed marble pillar placed atop an inverted Ionic pier-column capital, which served as a base.[4] Of the other three supports, all that survives are three large Asiatic Ionic column bases set at 2.93 m intervals. While the inner colonnade was clearly built later than the back wall and pier, its structural role in the portico remains unclear. The quantity and variety of tiles recovered from the collapsed debris suggest that it may have supported a

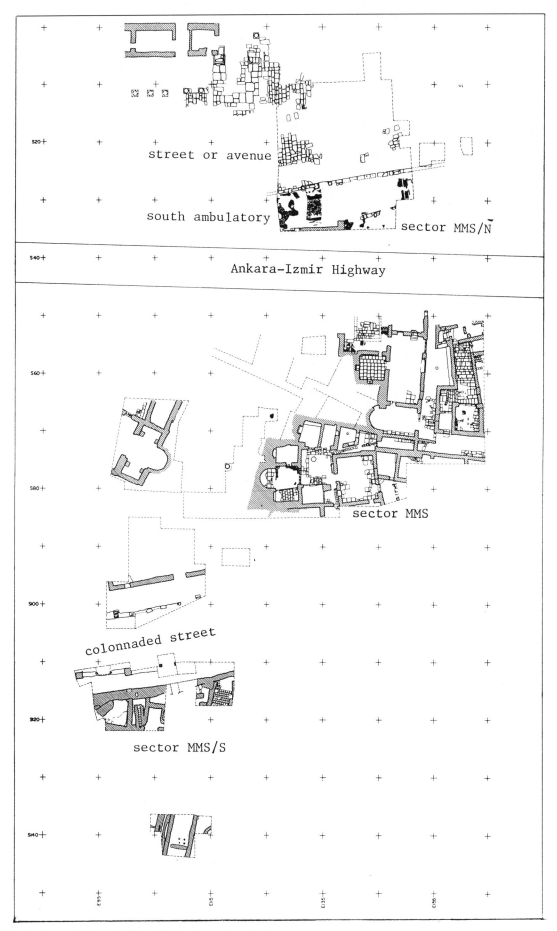

street or avenue

south ambulatory

sector MMS/N

Ankara–Izmir Highway

sector MMS

colonnaded street

sector MMS/S

Fig. 3. Sectors MMS, MMS/N, MMS/S, Roman levels, plan.

Fig. 4. Sector MMS/N, colonnaded ambulatory looking east; with lower mosaic floor, tile fall, and (far right), pier projecting from back wall.

large marble blocks, moldings, and column-shaft parts. Some of those fragments belonged to the street colonnade[5] or the south-lying structure, while others may have been intended for structural reuse or lime burning nearby. The area of the outer sidewalk northeast of the projecting pier was covered with a dense tile fall that still preserves articulated sections of the superstructure of the portico (Greenewalt *et al.* 1983: figs. 13, 14). Together with recovered spouted and *opaion* roof tiles, traces of an upper floor suggest that a second story once stood above the inner colonnade. Further excavation of this debris may resolve questions concerning the superstructure and confirm the date of its collapse, which apparently occurred in the early seventh century C.E.[6]

MMS.   Sector MMS comprises the area immediately south of the modern highway. Ten years of excavation at that sector have uncovered extensive remains of a Late Roman residential quarter with houses and streets constructed on top of and partially cut into the debris of Colossal Lydian Structure. In 1988 and 1989 work was carried out in different parts of the complex, discussed separately, proceeding from east to west and from north to south.

Area 1. The most extensively explored part of the MMS area is the assemblage of spaces located in the northeast part of the sector, close to the highway. Excavation in 1988 focused on the latest building phases of the complex in the seven spaces extending east of the previous year's work (to E. 165 on the 'B' grid; Greenewalt 1990: 1–8). Those levels, which include the final phases of occupation and abandonment of the complex in the sixth and seventh centuries C.E., lie approximately 1.5–2.0 m below the present ground surface. While the general arrangement of those late spaces is fairly clear, matters of chronology and function require further excavation. As was found throughout the sector, finds from final occupation levels were sparse and fragmentary, evidently the result of the abandonment and despoliation of the buildings prior to their structural collapse.[7] Coins and pottery provide approximate dates in the fifth through early seventh centuries C.E. for activities in the area.

The partially explored spaces designated IV, V, and XV through XXI constitute various late phases of the complex. Unlike the smaller rooms found elsewhere in the sector (discussed as Area 2, *infra*), these spaces are relatively large and open in plan, and they appear better suited to ceremony

second story, which would have extended further south beyond the limits of excavation. No evidence for a back wall of this double colonnaded area was noted within the area explored.

Fragments of two apparently contemporary mosaics survive in both inner and outer ambulatory spaces. The outer sidewalk area preserves an eroded polychrome mosaic with a frame of double guilloche tendrils and interlocking circles; the eastern edge of this mosaic, which included a fragmentary dedicatory inscription, was noted further to the east (Greenewalt *et al.* 1983: fig. 16). The orientation of the exposed south and east borders apparently derives from the line of the inner colonnade. Traces of a similar mosaic are preserved at a slightly higher level south of the inner stylobate. No direct evidence was recovered to confirm or change the previously suggested late sixth century-C.E. date for this mosaic surface.

Shortly thereafter the entire ambulatory area was covered by a thick layer of collapsed debris. In the western section were found a number of

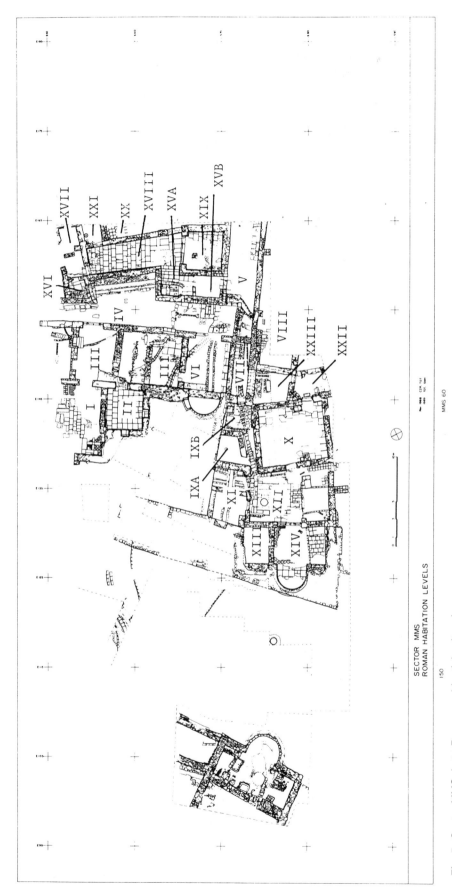

SECTOR MMS
ROMAN HABITATION LEVELS

MMS 60

150

Fig. 5. Sector MMS, Late Roman residential units, plan.

Fig. 6. Lead seal from sector MMS residential unit, obverse (left) and reverse (right): "(seal) of Kosmas the Deacon."

and display than to domestic routine. This public character is shared by the adjoining Rooms III and VI (Greenewalt *et al.* 1985: 68–73; Greenewalt, Rautman, and Meriç 1986: 4–5); considered together, these spaces suggest a formally structured dimension to their use in Late Roman times.

Spaces XVIII and XVA comprise the central architectural element of this area. Shaped by walls of varying dates and construction, these continuous spaces at one point formed an elongated, angled north-south corridor that connected almost all neighboring rooms (fig. 5). Its primary walls were sturdily built of mortared fieldstones with occasional brick bands and infrequent marble spoils. A relatively well preserved marble floor provided a uniform surface that sloped slightly at its north end toward two recessed drains. A low baseboard of marble revetment, set in mortar and fixed with iron pins, is preserved or attested around the perimeter of this long space. Space XVA is the L-shaped continuation from the southwest end of the 11 m long Corridor XVIII. Set in the outer corner of this appendage was the large water tank of which remains were uncovered in 1987 (Greenewalt 1990: fig. 7). That tank once would have formed a focus for the corridor, conspicuous to passersby approaching from Corridor XVIII to the east and through the doorway from Space XVB to the south.

Three or more spaces are clustered toward the north end of Corridor XVIII. The available area of study is limited by recent construction; the modern highway runs immediately to the north, and an electric cable was laid through the area in 1988. Only Room XVI is fully cleared; its small, squar-

ish plan with niches, bench-lined walls, and open doorway suggests a porter's booth near the north entrance to Corridor XVIII (Greenewalt 1990: 4–8, fig. 9). By this reasoning, Space XVII might have been a vestibule leading to Corridor XVIII, although subsequent alterations to the area obscure its original function. Still mostly unexamined is Space XXI, which opens through a doorway with threshold at the northeast corner of Corridor XVIII. The exposed sections of its north and west walls appear unfinished, and the space preserves only a hard-packed earthen floor. A stone mortar, 0.68 m high and 0.46 m in diameter, was found in the northwest corner and may reflect a late period of industrial activity. Further south, formerly accessible from Corridor XVIII by two doorways, is the large unexcavated Space XX, known only at its north end by its tile-paved floor.

The primary purpose of Corridor XVIII seems to have been to provide access to Room XIX, an almost square (4.4 × 4.0 m) space located at its south end. The room is enclosed on three sides by solid brick and rubble walls and preserves traces of a baseboard and marble floor. A 3.2 m wide opening on the north extends nearly the full width of the room and looks onto Corridor XVIII. The broad marble threshold of the door bears cuttings for several phases of use, which once may have included a grill or sliding shutters in addition to pivoting leaves. The wide doorway joining two marble paved spaces imparts an air of public ceremony to this area, an effect that would have been enhanced by the nearby presence of the large water tank in space XVA. The arrangement of rooms recalls domestic exedrae known from other Roman houses.[8]

A small lead sealing was recovered in the top preserved mortar bed of the south wall of Room XIX (M88.10/9595 = IN88.2). The observe bears a cross and the legend KOΣMA; the reverse presents two crosses and ΔIAKONOY in ligature (fig. 6). The apparent sixth-century context of the object attests a relatively early date at Sardis for this institution, which is thought to have spread from the east Mediterranean across the late empire in the mid-500s (Laurent 1965: 125–27). While the sealing alone is insufficient evidence to identify the MMS complex as a deaconry, it harmonizes with the resonant religious tenor of the quarter, with its cross-decorated wall painting, water tanks, and ceramics.[9]

The later history of these spaces is not fully clear. A small, poorly-built wall once partially closed off Space XVA from Corridor XVIII; a coin

Fig. 7. Sector MMS, Late Roman residential unit, Spaces IX–XIV (Area 2) in balloon photograph by E. E. and J. W. Myers taken in 1988 (before excavation of Rooms XXII and XXIII).

(tentatively assigned to Justinian I, 527–565 C.E.; 1988.109) recovered from its dry-laid rubblework suggests a sixth-century or later date for its construction. The broad doorway of Room XIX was narrowed to 1.4 m at one point, but later it was again cleared to its original width. The removal of paving and baseboard slabs in the western part of the room suggests that this room was quarried for building materials, even though Corridor XVIII was left relatively undisturbed. The bench that replaced the water tank in Space XVA may also date from this late phase of use (Greenewalt 1990: fig. 8). Contextual finds were limited primarily to animal bones and pottery of fifth and sixth century date.

This late phase of residential activity also appears in the further part of Space V exposed in 1988. Lying south of Spaces XVB and XIX, Space V forms a transitional element between other surrounding rooms (fig. 5). This 3.4 m wide space is still incompletely exposed but now extends at least 9.3 m east from its doorways to Space IV and Room XVB at its northwest end, with a 3.8 m spur projecting from its southwest corner. Its summarily finished state is clear from the irregular earthen surface and a clutter of exposed drains and pipes at its west end. Along the southeast part of the south wall extends a roughly flagged landing, from which at least three steps lead upward beyond the present limit of excavation. The unfinished condition of floor and walls gives the impression of a poorly maintained public space that offered access to rooms IV, VI, and III on the one hand, and to Space XV, Corridor XVIII, and Room XIX on the other. The series of spouted roof tiles noted in 1987 was found to continue along the exposed extent of the south wall, reinforcing the likelihood that either Space V or the unexplored space

Fig. 8. Sector MMS, Late Roman apsidal room (Area 3), looking west.

immediately to the south had been unroofed (Greenewalt 1990: 3–5). Relatively few roof tiles were recovered from Space V; but it preserves no arrangements for interior drainage (which one might expect if Space V were the unroofed of the two adjoining spaces). The poorly appointed condition of Space V resembles the steps and irregular paving of the adjoining Space IV. The proximity of such roughly finished transitional spaces to more elegantly furnished rooms is difficult to accept as part of the original design of the complex and more likely resulted from its late reorganization. As in Space IV, the latest identifiable coin from Space V apparently dates from the reign of Heraclius (1988.100: cf. Greenewalt 1990: 23 n. 8).

Area 2. The diversity of the sector in Late Roman times is shown by the more clearly domestic rooms located to the southwest. Excavation since 1980 has revealed a radially organized assemblage with a central court, an apsidal room, and surrounding domestic spaces (figs. 5, 7). Since previous work had established the north, west, and probably south boundaries of this complex, an effort was made in 1989 to clarify its eastern limits. A short campaign revealed a cluster of spaces adjacent to the residential core but did not resolve the question of its relationship with the other contemporary buildings discussed above. Only the latest occupied levels in this area were explored.

Space XXII opens through a 0.80 m wide doorway with threshold from the large tiled Room X to the west and through two further openings in its north wall (fig. 5). Both walls continue beyond the limits of excavation so the full dimensions of the space remain to be determined. As excavated, the floor consists of packed earth with a few scattered marble slabs set in pink mortar, below which extends a well constructed drain toward the east. The presence of deeper foundations suggests that the original appearance of the area may have been quite different. A fragmentary freestanding pier with vertical pipes indicates that the space may have been only partially roofed. A small oven or hearth is located in the northwest corner, between doorways in adjacent walls. Assembled of dry laid bricks and filled with abundant ash, the feature stands to a height of 0.70 m above floor level.

Two further rooms open from Space XXII through doorways in its north wall. The more westerly, Room XXIII, is trapezoidal in plan and measures ca. 3.5 × 4.5 m. At one time this room communicated directly with Room X through an opening in its west wall, which was blocked in a later phase of use. In its final phase, access to the room was possible only through the doorway with threshold from Space XXII. The only identified features of the partially excavated room are two large terracotta jars at floor level, covered by a stone slab (Greenewalt, Rautman, and Meriç 1986: 5). The adjacent room (VIII, unexcavated) also opened from Space XXII through a doorway that was blocked at a later time.

Area 3. A contemporary but independent group of spaces was identified in 1983 in the western part of the MMS sector. Earlier excavation had identified four related spaces cut into the western side of the hill (Greenewalt, Rautman, and Meriç 1986: 5–6). The two northernmost spaces appear to have been built in the fourth century C.E. and were occupied as late as the early 600s. In 1989 work was directed to clarifying the function and chronology of the more southern parts of this area.

The apsidal room is the largest space in the area. In plan it comprises an oblong trapezoid measuring ca. 3.5 × 9.0 m, oriented diagonally to the 'B' grid and approximately parallel to the line of Colossal Lydian Structure. On its southeast side is a broad semicircular apse that cuts into the pre-Roman strata of the hill (figs. 5, 8). The western limits are defined by a pair of projecting piers that embrace a 3.8 m wide opening to an adjacent space that continues beyond the present excavation limits. Both apse and piers may have been additions to an earlier rectangular space defined by the north and south walls; however, the apse apparently remained a feature of the room for most of the fifth and sixth centuries C.E.

The appearance of the apsidal room in this primary phase can be reconstructed from surviving fragments. Its walls, built of mortared rubble and bearing traces of painted plaster, still stand as much as 4 m high but preserve no traces of windows. The intact lower courses of the semidome suggest that the room may originally have risen to an interior height of over 6 m. The floor in this phase is known only from isolated patches of a coarse pink mortar that preserved impressions of marble paving. A large pipe once ran east to west beneath the floor but was partially removed in late antiquity. No evidence conclusively establishes the original function of the space.

The later history of the apsidal room is somewhat better known. At some point the marble paving was stripped, and a large pit was cut through the bedding at the center of the room. The floor was re-established with a rough terrazo-like surface of irregularly-cut, variegated marble fragments set in mud mortar, similar to the floor in one of the adjacent spaces to the north and elsewhere at the sector. At a still later time this floor was superceded by a series of packed earthen surfaces. Two sets of slender brick piers were added to opposite walls, creating a symmetrical pair of 1.4 × 3.5 m bays against the north and south walls. Later removed down to their lowest courses, these slender piers apparently served more to articulate the space than to reinforce its walls or roof. Shortly afterwards the appearance of the apsidal room was more drastically transformed (fig. 8). The broad west opening was mostly filled by a coarsely built rubble wall, leaving the room accessible only by a 1.2 m wide doorway with threshold block set on the south side. Two large shallow basins were set in the west and north parts of the room. With interior dimensions of 1.25 × 0.60 × 0.18 m and 0.85 × 0.62 × 0.15 m, both basins are surrounded by broad, flat rims and have a small drainage hole at one end. Such basins may have been used for fulling or dying textiles and reflect a functional change to industrial use. Other identified remains of this phase include a large lump of resinous material and a dense ash deposit in an inverted pithos set on a terracotta tile. Pottery and coins of Justin II support a later sixth-century date for this phase. Previous excavation demonstrated that the room remained open through the early reign of Heraclius.[10]

Well. A deep well at the crown of the MMS hillock, partially excavated in 1987, was cleared and studied. The cylindrical shaft continued to a total excavated depth of 24.2 m, where it ended with a stone-paved floor. While terracotta liners were found in the upper 9.7 m, the lower shaft was lined with brick and fieldstone. Much of the well was filled with dumped architectural and domestic debris, including several heavy deposits of large animal bones. The lowest levels yielded little pottery that can be regarded as use accumulation, and the shaft was apparently filled by two phases of deliberate dumping, first in the mid-to-late fifth century C.E., and again in the mid-to-late sixth century C.E. Pottery and coins provide a consistent chronological framework for tracing imported and locally produced vessels at the site (Rautman 1990).

MMS Street. The residential complex at sector MMS belongs to an urban block that was bounded on the south by a broad colonnaded street originating in the region of Sector HoB to the southwest. Isolated segments of both the north and south colonnades of the thoroughfare had been exposed in earlier years (the street proper rests directly under a modern village road). Excavation in the north ambulatory in 1988 and 1989 further clarified the sequence of architectural supports and verified an early fifth century C.E. date (Greenewalt, Cahill, and Rautman 1987: 18–20, fig. 4).

The north wall of the street was exposed between two openings identified in 1984. This 7.6 m section was of banded rubble construction and retained to the north both Lydian remains and domestic debris of the Late Roman period. This section of wall was dismantled to permit deeper excavation. As also seen further west, the north ambulatory presented a simple packed earth surface that sloped gently upward to the east. The irregularly mortared foundation of the colonnade stylobate follows this upward progression in a series of uneven steps. The colonnade lies not parallel to the north wall of the street, but angles toward it, narrowing from a maximum width of 4.3 m to 3.6 m at the east end of the explored area. In addition to the previously exposed pier and column, excavation in 1989 revealed a further three columns and a second pier set at 2.7–3.0 m intervals (figs. 9, 10), a sequence that mirrors the identified members of the south colonnade. On that evidence the appearance of the street can now be reconstructed with three sets of piers separated by groups of two or four paired columns. While the sequence of both colonnades may be symmetrical, their construction is not. The less well preserved columns to the south have slender monolithic shafts with Ionic bases left in quarry finish (Greenewalt et al. 1985: 76). The four northern columns are attested by two in situ and four toppled drums recovered at sidewalk level. Irregular in diameter and length, some if not all of them had been reused in the street colonnade.

The sloping surface of the north sidewalk has now been exposed for almost 18.0 m of its length. Its make-up consists of a series of closely superimposed occupation layers beginning with the creation of the street in the early fifth century C.E. As observed to the south, individual strata are rarely continuous over long distances and frequently appear punctuated by pits of intermittent plaster layers. Preserved within this sequence are at least two phases of collapse of the north wall and colonnade, including the small structure erected in the early sixth century C.E. at the excavated west end of the ambulatory. Further east, the emphatic deposit of up to 1.1 m of architectural debris signals the destruction of the colonnade with its north wall and the end of the use of the sidewalk in the mid- to late sixth century C.E. As previously observed, a massive Late Roman dump later covered much of the area.

The spaces that opened off the north sidewalk area remain poorly known. The narrow, more westerly doorway gave access to a roughly finished space cut out of the pre-Roman hillside. Excavation of this room identified only its west wall, which projects perpendicularly from the street wall. The space was surfaced with a cobble floor. The purpose of the broader eastern opening is more obscure. Situated immediately atop the partially robbed schist masonry of Colossal Lydian Structure, this opening apparently allowed access from the street to an irregularly sloping alleyway. Any finished surfaces or walls in the area were quarried in late antiquity, leaving a recessed hollow that was filled in with domestic refuse in the later fifth and sixth centuries A.D.

MMS/S. The south wall of the colonnaded street lies parallel to and 18.0 m distant from its counterpart. While its segmented construction had been noted earlier, little was known of its original function. In 1989 excavations were carried out in two parts of Sector MMS/S to clarify the wall and its relationship with the large hill rising behind it. The identified remains include mostly Lydian and Roman features that predate the construction of the street.

Like the north street wall, the south street wall retains to most of its preserved height pre-Roman strata including parts of Colossal Lydian Structure. The arched opening in the south wall (Greenewalt et al. 1983: 8; Greenewalt, Cahill, and Rautman 1987: 16–17) evidently led to a staircase that connected the south ambulatory with an upper level behind the street wall, where there is a Late Roman room (two steps of the upper end of the staircase were uncovered). Excavation of the area immediately behind the retaining wall revealed a dense group of walls at a level more than 7 m above the sloping roadway (fig. 9). Floor surfaces were either of packed earth or were absent, and the irregular faces of many of those walls suggest that they served as foundations for spaces whose upper parts no longer survive.

Despite their eroded, partially excavated state, the foundations attest a group of small rectilinear spaces flanking a narrow corridor or alleyway. Those walls are constructed of mortared rubble with little brick, but they also incorporate a few sculptural spoils, including a small marble Medusa head (S89.6/9722). Their footings step downward to the south and west and are supported by sloping layers of mixed gravel fill up to 3.0 m in depth. Contextual finds suggest that the development of the area took place relatively early in the Roman period, perhaps in the first or second centuries C.E.

This group of hillside buildings was apparently demolished before or at the time the colonnaded street was constructed in the early fifth century C.E. The northern ends of the walls were cut back and retained by the reinforced back wall of the street. Further west this reinforcing took the form of a series of contiguous masonry screens that step back as much as 4 m from the street. Problems of drainage

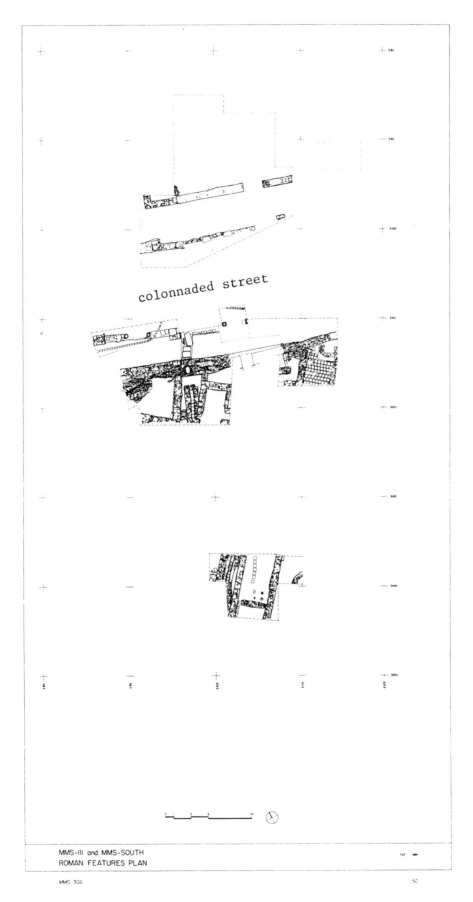

colonnaded street

MMS-III and MMS-SOUTH
ROMAN FEATURES PLAN

MMS-304

Fig. 9. Sectors MMS and MMS/S, Late Roman colonnaded street and Roman buildings to the south, plan.

were anticipated at the time, and a steep tile-covered channel was installed in the earlier corridor leading north from the upper hillside to a large drain behind the street wall. At street level this vertical chute emptied into a horizontal drain, which was identified in an earlier season (Greenewalt *et al.* 1983: 8). Another vertical drain, built of large terracotta pipes, is immured in the street wall 6 m further east.

To clarify the artificial hill south of the street, a trench was opened in 1989 ca. 30 m to the southeast, along the eastern slope of the hill. Excavation there revealed the lower parts of two parallel Late Roman walls running north to south with the contour of the hill (fig. 9). Rising from deep foundations, the western wall presents solid banded-rubble masonry faced with a grouted mortar surface. Like similarly constructed features at Sector MMS, this terrace wall originally supported higher ground to the west. A second, more slightly constructed wall stands 3.4 m further east and probably served a similarly retaining function.

The semicircular part of a mortared foundation was exposed to a height of over 2 m in the east end of the trench. Evidence for earlier Roman and Hellenistic occupation in this locale was recovered at lower levels, including four hypocaust tiles *in situ*, a tile floor, a row of tiles (from beneath which was recovered a coin of Constantius II [335–337 C.E.; C89.20]), and dense deposits of Hellenistic and early Roman pottery.

Perhaps at the time the retaining walls were constructed a tile-lined drainage channel was set into a narrow corridor running north. Poorly preserved traces of floors at that level, only a few centimeters below the present ground surface, suggest the occupation of the locale in the early fifth century C.E. (coin of Arcadius or Honorius, 394–408 C.E.; 1989.141). A still later pipe overlay the drainage channel, reflecting the continuing efforts of local residents to deal with the problems of water supply and drainage through late antiquity.

M.L.R.

Sectors MMS and MMS/S, Archaic Levels

Dominating both the locale and the research design since 1977 is a huge building of the Archaic period, Colossal Lydian Structure, parts of which are unusually well preserved. The Structure originally was 20 m thick and subsequently was made twice as thick by the addition of an earthwork, a glacis or *agger*; before the 1989 season, the Structure had been traced for 70 m, from the modern highway to the south. (The relationship of the Structure to contemporaneous monumental buildings north of the modern highway, in Sector MMS/N, remains unclear; no further Archaic material has been uncovered in that sector since 1984 (fig. 11; Greenewalt, Cahill, and Rautman 1987: 31–33; Ratté 1989: 22–23; Greenewalt 1989: 265). Massive, solid construction and steep sides indicate that Colossal Lydian Structure was a fortification of some kind. It was evidently built in the last quarter of the seventh century B.C.E. (Greenewalt 1979: 25). It was destroyed in the middle of the sixth century B.C.E., and the ruined superstructure (brick fall), which was dumped around the exterior at the time of destruction, preserved the truncated stump of the Structure as well as nearby ruins of a contemporaneous residential complex that had been destroyed at the same time. The destruction may be identified with the siege, capture, and partial sack of Sardis by Cyrus the Great of Persia between 547 and 542 B.C.E. (Cahill in Greenewalt, Cahill, and Rautman 1987: 28–29; Ramage 1986; below, and n. 17).

Between the destruction of Lydian buildings in the sixth century B.C.E. and Late Roman urbanization in the fifth century C.E. the history of occupation at Sectors MMS and MMS/S remains obscure. Late Roman construction may have removed features of the intermediate time period, of which little has been recovered in excavation (for slight features of the later sixth, fifth, and fourth centuries B.C.E. at Sector MMS, see Cahill in Greenewalt, Cahill, and Rautman 1987: 25–26; for Hellenistic and early Roman material at sector MMS/S, see Rautman, above). The only feature of this long intermediate period revealed at Sector MMS in 1988 and 1989 is part of an earthwork (distinct from the older glacis/*agger* earthwork cited in the preceding paragraph and below), which was piled over the ruined west side of Colossal Lydian Structure. Consisting of clayey earth with a small amount of burnt clay matter (from Brick Fall, see below), it has a maximum thickness of almost 3 m and is deposited in layers that incline to the west (fig. 12, section AA, upper left; Greenewalt *et al.* 1990: 169, n. 7). The latest diagnostic material that has been recognized from this earthwork consists of fragmentary "Achaemenid" pottery bowls, which suggest a date of deposit in the later sixth or early fifth century B.C.E.[11] The earthwork may have been created at about the same time as the "secondary limestone wall," built into the truncated stump of Colossal Lydian Structure (fig. 11; Greenewalt *et al.* 1983: 6, figs. 3, 6, 7).

Fig. 10. Sector MMS, Late Roman colonnaded street, north ambulatory, looking east.

Colossal Lydian Structure. Excavation aimed to clarify the design and two building phases of the west side, and the south continuation of the Structure (i.e., beyond ca. S. 115 on the 'B' grid, in sector MMS/S; cf. figs. 11, 3, 9). The reentrant corner exposed in 1985 (Greenewalt, Rautman, and Cahill 1987: 71; Greenewalt *et al.* 1990: 141, fig. 5, lower left) belongs to a bay or recess in the west side. The recess has symmetrically splayed sides; it is about 10 m deep, 8.15 m wide at the back, and 10.75 m wide in front (as far in front as it has been exposed; figs. 11, 12, 18). The back wall is older than the side walls and evidently represents the original west face of the Structure. The back wall extends beyond the reentrant corners and is aligned with segments of the original west face to the north: one segment exposed by the highway (Greenewalt *et al.* 1990: 141, fig. 5, top left), the other exposed 8–9 m north of the recess, in 1988.

In the narrow exposure 8–9 m north of the recess (at E. 112–113/S. 81–82 on the 'B' grid; fig. 18),

the west face had a sloped stone socle and mudbrick superstructure (the face of the latter now damaged or deteriorated). In design and materials it resembles the west face segment by the modern highway and contrasts with the back of the recess, which is vertical and built entirely of stone (as preserved). As has been observed, the east and west faces of the north part of the Structure are sloped and built with a stone socle and mudbrick superstructure, and the faces of the south part are vertical and built of stone (as preserved; Greenewalt, Cahill, and Rautman 1987: 21; Greenewalt 1989: 263). The changes in those design and construction systems occur in locations where the east and west faces have not been excavated (at ca. S. 70 on the 'B' grid for the west face and between ca. S. 82–91 for the east face).

The north wall of the recess retains the glacis/*agger* earthwork that was built against the original west face and that has been traced to the north as far as the modern highway (fig. 11; Greenewalt 1989: 263–64; Greenewalt *et al.* 1990: 141, figs. 4, 7, 8).

The south wall of the recess may have retained a similar earthwork: layers of sandy earth that are inclined to the west, like layers that form the earthwork north of the recess, were located 2–3 m south of the south wall and a little above the level of the south wall foot; and the south wall has the same distinctive plan, diminishing in thickness from east to west, as the north wall. An earthwork south of the recess would have extended for a distance of only 10 m, as far as the east-west wall located in that direction (fig. 11; for the wall, see Greenewalt, Rautman, and Meriç 1986: 8–9, figs. 11, 12).

The original height of the glacis/*agger* earthwork north of the recess, which still stands ca. 12 m high, is not known. That its surface inclined to the west is suggested by the consistent incline of its component layers, which would have provided weak support for a horizontal surface, and by the diminishing thickness of the retaining wall towards the west, which suggests that there was progressively less bulk to retain in that direction.

The recess walls are best preserved near the northeast corner. The north wall stands to a maximum preserved height of 3.8 m and contains the socket for a horizontal wood beam, 2.35–2.80 m above the recess floor and aligned with the wall face (figs. 14, 17).[12] To the south and west the walls stood only one-to-two courses high, the upper parts having been removed partly in the sixth or fifth century B.C.E. (at the southwest end) and in Late Roman times (during construction of the colonnaded street, see above). Bottom courses of the south wall (the only directly attested courses) were built of polygonal and ashlar blocks of limestone and sandstone: a unique instance of neatly fitted masonry and a rare instance of limestone in Colossal Lydian Structure.

The glacis/*agger* earthwork north of the recess was created sometime between the construction of Colossal Lydian Structure in the last quarter of the seventh century B.C.E. and its destruction in the middle of the sixth century B.C.E. (Greenewalt 1990: 10–11; for previous uncertainty, see Greenewalt *et al.* 1990: 143). L. E. Stager has suggested that it might have been created to protect the Structure from mining and sapping, like earthworks that were adjuncts of Bronze Age fortifications in Palestine and Syria and like the Late Roman walls at Dura Europos. Since the destruction of the Structure may be identified with the capture of Sardis by Cyrus the Great in the 540s, and since sapping and mining operations are well attested for Achaemenid Persian siege warfare,

Stager's suggestion is consistent with the presumed historical context of the glacis/*agger* earthwork, which might have been created in anticipation of Cyrus's attack.[13]

The destruction of Colossal Lydian Structure is attested by two strata within the recess: an upper stratum of fieldstones and small boulders, one to three stones thick, and a lower stratum of Brick Fall. The stony stratum apparently consists of stones that had belonged to the packing of the recess walls (Greenewalt 1990: 10, and fig. 12), and it may have been deposited after the Structure was destroyed, when larger stones of the recess wall facing were removed for reuse elsewhere, and smaller stones of the packing spilled out or were pulled into the recess.

Immediately above and below the stony layer, two narrow earthy strata were identified by excavator N. D. Cahill. They might be accumulation that reflects time intervals between the deposit of the stony stratum and the clayey earthwork above, and the deposit of the stony stratum and of the Brick Fall below.[14]

The stratum of Brick Fall (consisting primarily of semibaked reddish and unbaked greenish gray brick fragments; see Cahill in Greenewalt, Cahill, and Rautman 1987: 22–24) filled the recess. On the north side the deposit was preserved to its original top surface, which inclined to the west, away from the inner end of the recess (figs. 12, 13).

The Brick Fall on the east side of the Structure also inclined away from the Structure face (Greenewalt, Cahill, and Rautman 1987: fig. 7; Greenewalt *et al.* 1990: figs. 4 [left], 6 [inset]). The incline may have been created deliberately rather than the result of haphazard spillage. Within the recess the Brick Fall deposit may have been designed to approximate the glacis/*agger* earthwork, to provide, with the earthwork, a foundation for the post-destruction clayey earthwork (above).

Although substantially removed in the south part of the recess (like the recess walls, above), some Brick Fall deposit remained *in situ* over all of the recess floor. The Brick Fall in the recess contained a larger proportion of semibaked brick fragments than that on the east side of the Structure,[15] and a number of severely burned and blistered brick fragments, which are not attested in Brick Fall on the east side. Cahill, the excavator, has attributed most of the semibaking to deliberate (partial) firing by the brick makers, and the severe burning and blistering to the mid-sixth-century destruction. The

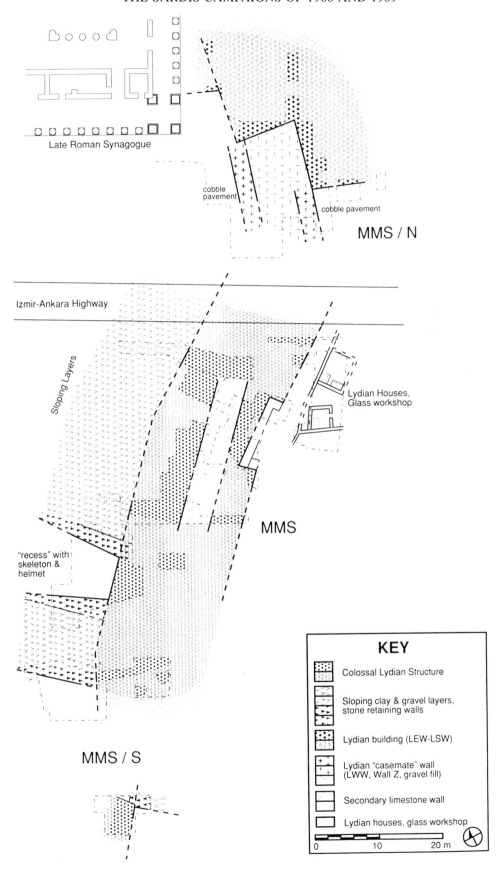

Fig. 11. Sectors MMS, MMS/N, and MMS/S, Archaic levels, schematic plan.

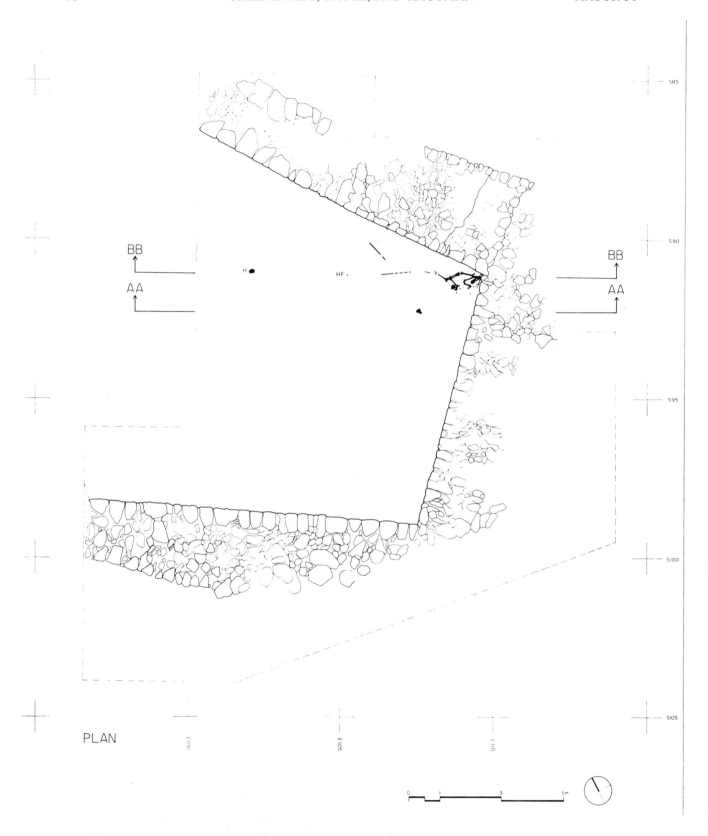

Fig. 12. Colossal Lydian Structure, west side: recess, plan and sections showing relationship of Brick Fall, human skeleton, and helmet. Section AA shows Brick Fall (the same section that appears in fig. 13, reversed) and clayey

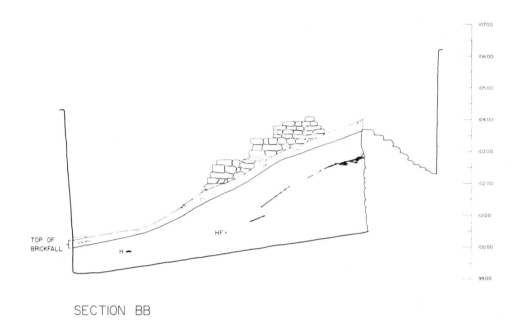

SECTION BB

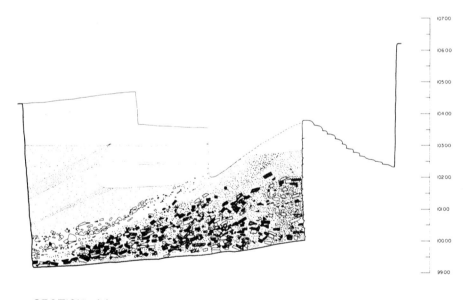

SECTION AA   (REVERSED FROM SCARP DRAWING)

earthwork (at upper left). Section BB shows skeleton and helmet (H = fragments recovered in 1987; HF = fragment recovered in 1988).

Fig. 13. Colossal Lydian Structure, west side: recess, looking south. The picture shows a section through Brick Fall, which has been removed in the north side of the recess, and the surface of Brick Fall in the south side of the recess. In the background are foundations, column drums, and a pier of the north colonnade of the Late Roman street.

Brick Fall in the recess must have been deposited at the same time as that on the east side of the Structure and further to the north and south, about the middle of the sixth century B.C.E.[16]

Brick Fall within the recess excavated in 1988 and 1989 contained the skeleton of a mature man, a small fragment of an iron and bronze helmet (of which substantial parts had been recovered in 1987), and remains of two slender wood items (Greenewalt 1990: 11-3; Greenewalt and Heywood 1992; Greenewalt 1992).

The skeletal remains (almost all excavated in 1988) rested about 0.75 m below the Brick Fall surface, in the northeast corner of the recess; the left pelvis (excavated in 1989) rested apart, about 2 m from the left femur head (figs. 14–16). Some skeletal parts were articulated: bones of both legs, both arms, and of the head, neck, and upper torso. The position of the skeletal ensemble suggested to M. R. Domurad that the body had fallen or been hurled from above, landing head-first (the skull rested upside down and under some of the ribs).

The cause of separation of the leg and left arm bones from the torso remains unclear. Domurad thought that those parts probably became separated after deposit, as a result of Brick Fall settling, rather than before or at the time of deposit, as a result of mutilation or decay. The amount of leg displacement is considerable, however, and contrasts with the articulation of the leg bones. On the other hand, the clutched position of the right-hand thumb and finger bones around a stone (fig. 16; see also below) could hardly have been sustained after leg amputation, and suggests that deposition of the body occurred before the flesh and sinew were sufficiently decayed to release the leg and arm bones.[17]

Domurad estimated that the skeleton belonged to a man 22–26 years old, 1.75–1.77 m tall and in good health and physical condition at the time of death. That he had been a soldier is suggested by evidence for muscular development of his arms, the left arm developed for supporting weight like that of a shield ("particularly pronounced deltoid

Fig. 14. Colossal Lydian Structure, west side: northeast corner of recess, looking north, with human skeleton in Brick Fall.

tuberosity on the left humerus"), the right arm for "repetitive forward motion or rotation, such as might be necessary in sword use" ("extra lipping of the right glenoid cavity"); by evidence for regular pressure on the head of weight like that of a helmet ("all the cervical vertebrae displayed flattening and compression deformation"); and by two head wounds, of kinds that "occur frequently in other skeletons of military participants," sustained some three to four years before death.[18] Although those features could have other explanations, their combined occurrence strongly suggests a military one. Furthermore, the helmet remains recovered in 1987 and 1988 belonged to the same context: they rested on the same incline of Brick Fall as the skeleton, and one fragment (recovered in 1988) rested about midway between the main cluster of fragments (recovered in 1987) and the skeleton, 2.75 m distant from the latter (fig. 12). Whether the man had been the actual owner or wearer of the helmet, however, is uncertain: no other metal armament was closely associated with the skeleton.[19] A stone, smooth and about the size of an apricot, which was held between the clutched thumb and finger bones of his right hand, might signify that the man had been an army slinger or stone-thrower, but it could just as plausibly reflect a special situation (Greenewalt and Heywood 1992: 5, 22 n. 9; Greenewalt 1992: 260 nn. 19, 20). He evidently died in violent circumstances, attempting to defend himself, as is attested by left forearm bone fractures that were sustained just before death

when the arm was in a raised, defensive position.[20] In the suggested interpretation of Brick Fall destruction, the man may be identified as a soldier of either Croesus or Cyrus; he apparently died during Cyrus's siege or capture of Sardis and his remains, like the helmet, were unceremoniously deposited in the destruction debris.

The helmet fragment belongs to a tongue of the finial (Greenewalt 1990: 11–13; Greenewalt and Heywood 1992: 7). The two wood items are attested by "ashy" material and by impressions in the Brick Fall; one might have been a spear (fig. 12).[21]

The Brick Fall deposit rested on the floor of the recess (fig. 17), which was a surface of small cobbles overlaid by a thin layer of earthy material. The floor was practically bare of artifacts,[22] apart from about 70 iron nails (including some 25 excavated in 1987; Greenewalt 1990: 12). Most of the nails were arranged in four or five "grid sets" (fig. 18). The sets are evidently vestiges of panels of wood slats, secured by nails, which had rested flat on the recess floor. The panels might have fallen from above, and they might have been doors or shutters (for windows, embrasures?) in the superstructure of Colossal Lydian Structure.

The nails are 0.10–0.13 m long. Most of their pointed ends are clenched over. There were three grid sets in the range of a meter square (1.3 × 1.0 m; 0.95 × 0.8 m; 1.04 × 0.9 m); all three had three to five nails per row, two sets with three rows, one with four rows. A fourth set (excavated in 1987) was longer and narrower: 2.3 × 0.45 m, with

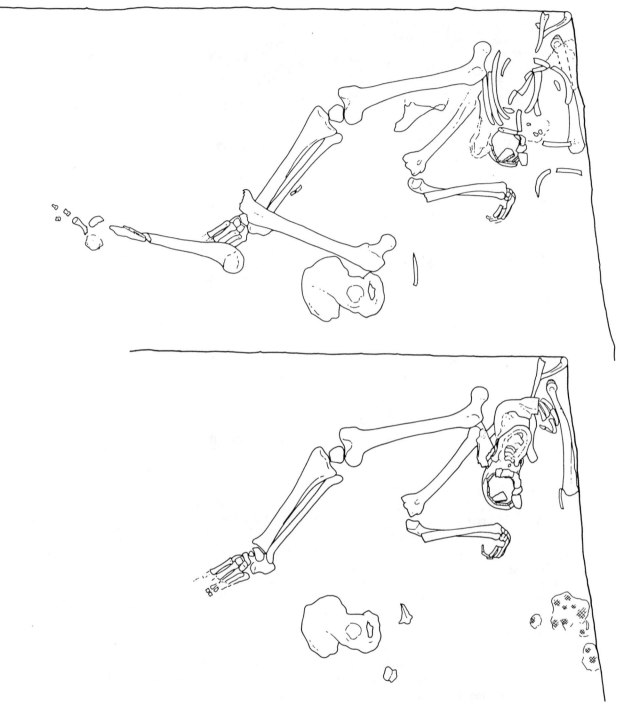

Fig. 15. Human skeleton in northeast corner of recess, west side of Colossal Lydian Structure: above, with uppermost bones; below, with uppermost bones removed (drawings by C. S. Alexander).

three rows of eight to nine nails per row. Of a possible fifth set, only four nails were recovered (near the south side of the recess). Almost all nails *in situ* had a vertical orientation. In two of the smaller sets the nails were pointed-end up; in the third, and per-

haps also in the large set, they were head-end up. Wood pseudomorphs adhered to many nails, and traces of wood were recovered along one edge of one set. Excavator Cahill suggests that the panels consisted of slats and crossbars, "e.g., four slats held together by three cross-bars" (N. D. Cahill, 1989, sector MMS-III Final Report manuscript, 14). For windows of comparable sizes in Greek fortifications of the fourth century B.C.E. and Hellenistic period, see Lawrence 1979: 406; for window shutters, Lawrence 1979: 410–18.

South Continuation of Colossal Lydian Structure. Up to 1989 Colossal Lydian Structure had been traced 65 m south of the modern Ankara-Izmir highway, where its substructure is exposed below foundations of the Late Roman colonnaded street (see above; at ca. S. 110–115 on the 'B' grid, in sector MMS/S; Greenewalt *et al.* 1983: 8–10; Greenewalt *et al.* 1985: 78; Greenewalt, Rautman, and Meriç 1986: 8–9). The Structure clearly continues further south, since its substructure extends beyond the south limits of exposure (i.e., under the south wall of the Roman street). Beyond that point is an artificial hill, and the Structure remains had been understood to rest under massive Roman overburden.[23]

A small test trench opened in 1989 directly behind the south wall of the Roman street,[24] however, exposed coursed mudbrick construction *in situ* only 1 m below modern ground surface. That the construction belonged to Colossal Lydian Structure seemed self-evident; adjacent mixed fill also contained several Archaic pottery fragments (e.g., "subgeometric" skyphos with nicked rim). To clarify the form and extent of the Structure south of the Roman street, two larger trenches were opened, one immediately behind the south wall of the Roman street, the other some 30 m further south, on the east slope of the artificial hill (fig. 11; on Roman levels of sector MMS/S for which see above).

The trench behind the south wall of the Roman street exposed much Roman construction; and, in one small open space (ca. 2 m × 3.8 m) an uncontaminated Archaic stratum of earthy debris with inclusions of mudbrick fragments and fragmentary pottery of standard Lydian types. The trench ca. 30 m further south (T-shaped; at the bottom of the plan in fig. 11) exposed part of a monumental stone building, against which rests a deposit of what appears to be Brick Fall destruction debris (fig. 19).

The facade is oriented north-south and faces east; it is built of large, roughly-dressed blocks of schist and quartzite. The segment exposed in 1989 is nearly 3 m long and 16 courses high. Neither the bottom nor a "floor" was exposed. The top-preserved two or three courses are somewhat displaced. The

Fig. 16. Human skeleton from recess: right forearm and hand bones, with thumb and finger bones clutched around stone. Above, in similar position for comparison, right hand of 22–26 year-old modern Sardian.

stone packing behind the facade is partly disturbed, by both Roman and Archaic construction; the latter includes a crude "face," oriented east-west and facing north (in the north end of the trench).

Evidently associated with the Archaic internal alteration is a construction that replaced part of the facade and extends to the east of it. This construction has a face to the south oriented east-west, built of small, neatly-cut blocks of sandstone (exposed to a height of 1.4 m; fig. 19 shows the top-preserved stones, seen from above). From Archaic fills behind this adjunct and in front of the internal alteration "face" were recovered fragments of a Late (?) Corinthian aryballos of "subgeometric style" (P89.51/9691; for the type, see Payne 1931: 321, fig. 162) and of an Attic Siana(?) cup (P89.52/ 9692), which suggest a *terminus post quem* of the first quarter of the sixth century B.C.E. for the date of the alteration of the main facade and the building of the adjunct.

Resting against the main facade and the adjunct face, and overlapping top stones of the latter, is a deposit of fragmentary brick, some fragments unfired and some semibaked, and random fieldstones, all disposed in strata that incline from the

Fig. 17. Colossal Lydian Structure, west side: recess, looking northeast.

main facade (fig. 19, visible in the trench scarp at left). This deposit appears to be Brick Fall. It is clearly later than both the main facade and the adjunct, and it may be connected with the burning on the top stones of the latter.

The built stone features evidently belong to Colossal Lydian Structure and represent two phases of construction, both anterior to the mid-sixth century B.C.E. destruction if the deposit with fragmentary brick is Brick Fall. The main facade may be the east face of the Structure; and the east slope of the artificial hill, which has approximately the same orientation and which extends for a total distance of ca. 60 m, to a point ca. 130 m south of the modern Ankara-Izmir highway, may reproduce the line of that face and indicate its location and extent.

Residential Complex. East of Colossal Lydian Structure, in the residential complex that had been destroyed at the same time as the Structure and had been buried under Brick Fall from the Structure (Cahill in Greenewalt *et al.* 1990: 143–55 and references), there was no major excavation in 1988

and 1989. However, a small salvage excavation took place in the occupation stratum of the mid-sixth century B.C.E. east of the "yard" zone; several pottery items from 1986 excavations were restored (fig. 20) or repaired and inventoried,[25] and the human skeletal remains recovered from the floor of the "yard" zone in 1966 were studied by M. R. Domurad. She reports:

The human remains . . . are from a male, aged 35–40 years at death. . . . No bones were sufficiently complete to determine stature. . . . The build of the individual was rather slight, with stronger legs than arms. The left elbow (distal humerus, proximal radius and ulna) shows signs of some stress, and there is moderate osteoporotic resorption near most joints. The spine shows notable arthritic development, as well as at least three Schmorl's nodes. The fingers also show a moderate amount of degenerative arthritis. No other pathological conditions were evident.

The indicators of stress and degeneration suggest that the individual was involved in strenuous and repetitive bending, lifting, or carrying weight on the back (M. R. Domurad, 1989, Human Bones Report manuscript, 6).

Fig. 18. Colossal Lydian Structure, west side: plan, showing position of iron nails just above the floor of the recess; and exposure of older west face, to the north.

Fig. 19. South continuation of Colossal Lydian Structure in Sector MMS/S, looking west: facade, with adjunct construction at lower right, and Brick Fall (?) in scarp at left.

How this person died and why his remains rested in the residential complex remain a mystery. Mutilation or scavenging by animals had previously been suggested as possible explanations for the absence of some skeletal parts (Cahill in Greenewalt *et al.* 1990: 150). Domurad's study produced no further evidence to support or reject mutilation. No cut marks were observed on the bones. Many bones had been recovered incomplete and in partly deteriorated condition.[26] The skeletal remains are unlikely to have rested for long in the residential complex before the complex was destroyed, and the complex must have been buried under Brick Fall soon after it was destroyed.

C.H.G.

SECTOR BYZFORT

Sector ByzFort is the flat-topped hill or spur that projects from the north side of the Acropolis,

like a promontory overlooking the Hermus plain (at ca. E. 630–730/S. 310–460 on the 'B' grid; fig. 1, B; fig. 2, no. 23). Trenches dug between 1983 and 1987 into the north and east sides of the hill revealed sections of the face of a great platform or terrace, apparently built in the mid- or late-sixth century B.C.E. Trenches dug in 1985 and 1986 on top of the hill uncovered a Roman building of early Imperial date; excavation beneath Roman floor levels in parts of that building revealed some earlier features, including a large stone foundation that seems to predate the great Archaic terrace. In 1988 and 1989, work continued in two areas: in a new trench in the east side of the hill, and in those parts of the Roman building on top, where pre-Roman strata had not been fully examined (for results of previous work, see Greenewalt *et al.* 1990: 155–62 and references).

East Side

Roughly halfway between the northeast corner of the Archaic terrace and the southernmost exposed section of the face of the terrace, a concave dip or depression, resembling the *cavea* of a theater, interrupts the steep east side of the ByzFort hill (at E. 718–722/S. 416–426 on the 'B' grid; fig. 21). In two months of excavation in 1988 and 1989, a 4 m × 10 m trench was dug into its south side, in the hope of determining whether it was a natural or manmade feature, and if manmade, whether or not it was contemporary with the Archaic terrace and concealed a road or stairway leading to the top of the terrace.

Roman Features. Excavation quickly revealed a large retaining wall, roughly built of mortared sandstone blocks and fieldstones, running across the south end of the trench (fig. 22). A second wall runs 6 m to the north, parallel to the first wall, but freestanding (fig. 23). Between those two walls, a series of floor surfaces was encountered at levels 5.0 m to 5.5 m below the top of the large retaining wall. A doorway (later blocked) through the freestanding wall gave access to the area; fragments of two reused columns suggest that it was roofed. The lowest floor concealed a system of waterworks including several pipes and a settling basin; pottery and coins found between and beneath the floors belong to the late fourth and fifth centuries C.E.[27]

Pre-Roman Features. Excavation beneath Roman floor levels showed that the retaining wall in

Fig. 20. Boat-shaped vessel from Lydian residential complex (P86.15/ 9223), recovered in 1986, restored in 1988 and 1989.

the south end of the trench rests on top of a massive oblong foundation (fig. 22). This foundation is made of sandstone blocks, laid in mud mortar and chinked with flakes of sandstone and limestone; presumably it is the original source of the sandstone blocks (reused) in the later retaining wall. Approximately 3 m wide, the sandstone foundation projects from the south and east sides of the trench, but stops short of the northerly (freestanding) Roman wall, which is founded on bedrock.

At its northwest corner, the sandstone foundation also rests on bedrock; elsewhere, the bedrock slopes down across the middle of the trench to the east and down along the west side of the trench to the south, and the foundation rests on fill. No datable artifacts were recovered from the earth packed up against the sandstone foundation, but the closest parallels for the construction technique belong to the Archaic and Classical periods.[28]

Conclusions. The two Roman walls both run east-west, parallel to the modern topographical contours. The area north of the space between those walls may have been occupied by an open-air alley or a street. Thus the depression or concavity in the east side of the ByzFort hill does seem to have been created at least in part by manmade structures, which may have incorporated a passageway to the top of the hill. The topographical change, however, need not have occurred before Roman times, when the retaining wall was built— it may date to Late Roman times.

The sandstone foundation beneath the retaining wall may be contemporary with or even earlier than the Archaic terrace. The contours of the bedrock

beneath the foundation suggest that when the foundation was built, the topography of the surrounding area was very different from its present state. It is possible that the foundation belonged to some sort of bastion on the south side of the modern concavity; but for the present, both the purpose of the foundation and the pre-Roman topography of that part of Sector ByzFort are matters for conjecture.

Spur Summit

Archaic Features. Excavation on the top of the hill concentrated on the area defined by the northern half of the Roman building (fig. 24). The area consisted of two rooms, both about 7 m by 7 m square, separated by a narrow corridor, 1.75 m wide; excavation in 1985 and 1986 had already exposed Archaic levels in the easterly square room and Archaic or Hellenistic levels in the westerly square room and in the central corridor. In one month of work in 1989, the Roman corridor walls and the remaining post-Archaic strata were removed, until the whole area had been dug to Archaic levels or bedrock.

In the center of this area, beneath the floor of the Roman corridor, excavation revealed a narrow foundation, comprising a square marble plinth flanked by paving stones of marble and sandstone (fig. 25). The paving stones are smooth on top, but a rough-picked circular patch on top of the plinth shows that this was meant to bear a column. The ground surface south of this foundation, or stylobate, seems to have been level with the top of the paving stones; the dressing of the north face of the stylobate suggests that to the north the ground surface was some

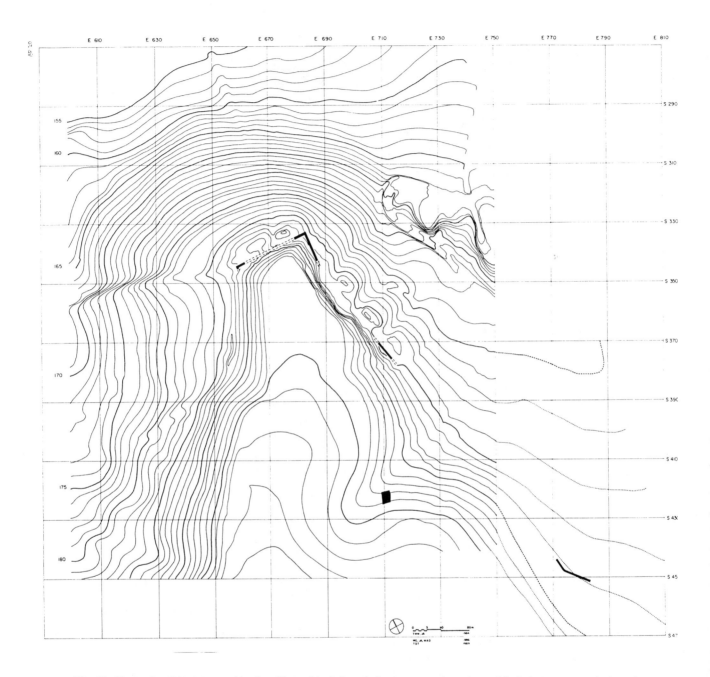

Fig. 21. Sector ByzFort, topographic plan. Heavy black lines indicate exposed sections of Archaic terrace, and of sandstone foundation in concavity in east side of hill.

0.1 m lower. Thus the stylobate may have acted as a kind of threshold, approached from the north.

To the east, the stylobate was cut by the east wall of the Roman corridor; to the west, it has been robbed out, but the robber's trench suggests that it originally extended at least 3–4 m further. The robber's trench was filled with several large chunks of stone, including fragments of a second

marble column plinth and of a limestone paving block. The masonry of the stylobate, especially the absence of claw-chisel marks, suggests a date in the sixth century B.C.E. or earlier (Nylander 1970: 49–56; Stronach 1978: 99–100).

Excavation north of the stylobate, below its foundation level, revealed a series of four overlapping pits dug into bedrock. The deepest and earliest,

Fig. 22. Sector ByzFort, view of trench in concavity in east side of hill, looking north.

Fig. 23. Sector ByzFort, view of trench in concavity in east side of hill, looking south.

cut by the other three, seems to have been the basement of a freestanding structure. It is rectangular in plan, oriented roughly north-south, with large circular postholes in its northwest corner (the only corner exposed) and along its north and west sides. The stylobate rests partly on the fill of this basement.

Pottery recovered from the fills of both the basement and the later pits composes a rich and relatively uniform assemblage. Those fills have still not been entirely excavated, but a preliminary examination shows three main categories of vessels: large geometric jars (at least ten); plain, geometric, and orientalizing stemmed dishes (about 40); and gray monochrome dishes and pots (as many as 70). The nature of this assemblage suggests domestic occupation; compare the assemblage from the Archaic residential complex at sector MMS, which was much richer and which also included large numbers of stemmed dishes (Greenewalt *et al.* 1990: 148–49; Greenewalt, Cahill, and Rautman 1987: 27–28). Some of the dishes are illustrated in fig. 26; local parallels sug-

gest a date in the mid- or late seventh century B.C.E. (Hanfmann 1983: 28–29 presents parallels from sector HoB, "Lydian Level II").

East of and partly overlapping the basement lies the large stone foundation uncovered in 1985 and 1986. North and west of the basement, the bedrock has been leveled off at an elevation of 192.2 m above sea level: 0.5 m below the top of the stylobate, and 2.3 m above the floor of the basement. This bedrock platform was cut by an assortment of shallow pits and trenches of uncertain function.

Conclusions. Archaic occupation at the north end of the ByzFort hill seems to fall into three phases from the mid-seventh to the mid-sixth century B.C.E. The first phase is represented by the rectangular basement in the center of the hill and the second by the large stone foundation east of the basement; the leveling of the bedrock around those features may belong to either of the first two phases. The third phase is represented by construction of the great Archaic terrace. The stylobate

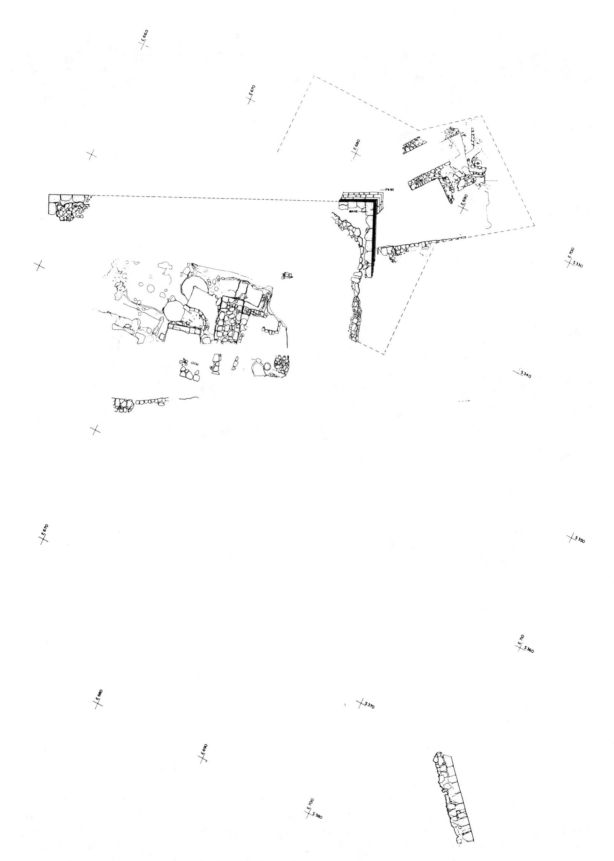

Fig. 24. Sector ByzFort, spur summit, plan of Lydian features.

Fig. 25. Sector ByzFort, spur summit, Archaic stylobate, looking south.

uncovered in 1989 presumably belongs to one of the last two phases, but to which is unclear. In either case, this stylobate is the first attested example of marble masonry in the civic architecture of Lydian Sardis, and the only certain instance of ashlar masonry in any Archaic monument other than a tomb or terrace wall.[29]

C.R.

GRAVES AT SARDIS AND BIN TEPE

In the city cemetery of Sardis west of the Pactolus stream (in the locale "Haci Oğlan," north of the Necropolis massif; fig. 1, C; Hanfmann 1962: 4, fig. 1, "t3") a stone-built chamber tomb and ten sarcophagus burials were excavated in 1989: the chamber tomb by the Expedition (to gain more information about funeral architecture and to provide experience for novice excavators), and sarcophagus burials by the Archaeological and Ethnographical Museum in Manisa (as a salvage project, after the sarcophagi had been uncovered in earth-moving operations aimed at agricultural development). At Bin Tepe, across the Hermus River plain, two graves were excavated by the Manisa Museum.

Chamber Tomb at Sardis

According to local reports, the existence of the tomb, Tomb 89.11, has been known for a long time. Before excavation, ceiling blocks of the main chamber were visible; a hole created by the missing end of one ceiling block permitted access to the main chamber, which was one-half to two-thirds filled with earthy debris. Excavation revealed an antechamber and dromos in addition to the main chamber, and exposed the interiors of both chambers, the tops of their ceiling blocks, and the inner end of the dromos (figs. 27, 28). The ensemble presumably had once been covered by a tumulus.[30] General design and construction features are characteristic of tumulus tombs at Sardis and elsewhere in Lydia.

The tomb is built of conglomerate, sandstone, and limestone. The main chamber had a floor of plaster, and interior wall surfaces of the main chamber and antechamber were covered with lime plaster. The dromos is open; the antechamber had a flat ceiling of three slabs (conglomerate), the main chamber a double-pitched ceiling of four slabs (limestone), two resting lengthwise on either side of the ridge. The two doorways, between the dromos and antechamber and between the antechamber and main chamber, had each been closed with a single door stone (limestone), with rebated top and sides to fit the (exterior) door frames (the outer door block is *in situ*; the inner block was found resting on its front surface in the antechamber).

Stones of the main chamber in general are larger and more neatly cut and joined than those of the antechamber. Some stones are rather large; notably the ceiling beams of the main chamber, over 3 m long, and the tympanum block between the main chamber and the antechamber, 2.18 m long. Walls of the main chamber show some rabbet joints; and at the ceiling ridge the joining surface of one beam is recessed to receive the other. In both chambers

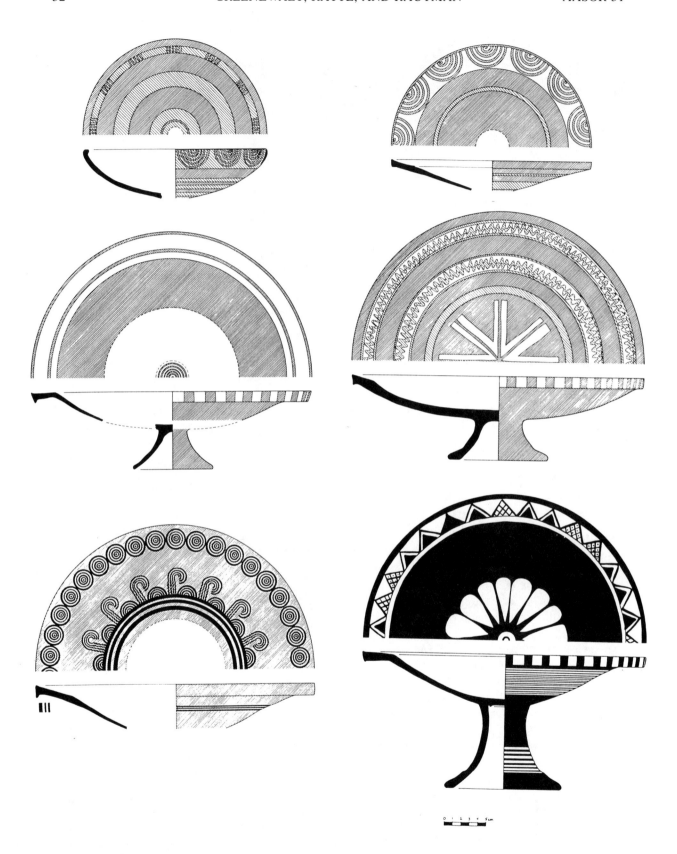

Fig. 26. Stemmed dishes from sector ByzFort. Top row, left to right, P89.64/9707 and P89.62/9705. Middle row, P89.63/9706 and P89.47/9684. Bottom row, P89.65/9708 and P86.59/9292=P89.39/9673.

there is some chinking with small stones, and there is no evidence in any part for clamps and dowels. The dromos walls (as exposed) are made of crudely cut and joined stones.

The main chamber has three benches, two on each side and one at the back, their undersides ca. 1.3 m above the floor in the center of the chamber. Each bench is a single slab of limestone, the upper surface of which has been hollowed to create a rectangular trough 0.15–0.26 m deep. The benches are supported by an interlock system with the chamber walls and with one another: the back bench ends are socketed into the side walls; the front ends of the side benches are socketed into the front wall of the chamber, and the flanged lips of their back ends rest on the front side of the back bench, where the edge of the trough has been lowered to receive them. Below the three benches the plaster floor is recessed to form a rectilinear U-shaped channel, as wide as the benches and 0.15 m deep. The chamber thus has "double-decker bunks" that could accommodate six interments, three in the benches above, three in the corresponding channel below.

A limestone slab resting at floor level in the antechamber (fig. 28) is evidently reused. The slab is rectangular except for a narrow rounded projection at one corner; the projection has a scalloped outline that resembles an asymmetrical palmette antefix of Archaic style. An adjacent corner is broken and could have had a similar projection. Might the slab have been intended to be a stele crowned on both sides by a pair of palmette-like ornaments? The other end of the slab is cut to fit into the doorway between the antechamber and the main chamber.

The different orientation of the main chamber and antechamber presumably reflects two construction phases (whether the antechamber abuts or bonds with the main chamber is unclear because of concealing wall plaster); there need not have been a significant time lapse between phases. Differences in orientation, chinking, imprecise joints, and the use of coarse-grained conglomerate are uncharacteristic of tumulus tomb chambers of the sixth century B.C.E. at Sardis and elsewhere in Lydia. Those features bespeak a more casual attitude toward design and construction than was common in the sixth century; but they would not have been conspicuous when the tomb was finished since the differences in orientation are obvious only in a surveyed plan, and the other features were concealed by interior plaster. Double-pitched ceilings and

Fig. 27. Haci Oğlan, Tomb 89.11: exterior, looking north.

three benches (in the same arrangement as those in Tomb 89.11) are attested for some tumulus chambers and are common in rock-cut tombs of the city cemetery. Double-pitched ceilings are evidently not a feature of the earliest tumulus chambers. Benches are normally lower and supported from underneath, either as part of a solid bedrock counter or using separate supports; the interlock support arrangement of Tomb 89.11 benches is unusual, and together with their greater height presumably is connected with the use of space underneath for interments.[31]

Although thoroughly rifled, probably more than once, Tomb 89.11 yielded a fair amount of human bone, pottery, and lamp fragments, most of which were recovered from the lower resting places of the main chamber and all in contexts of some disturbance. One relatively discrete bone assemblage (from the northeast corner of the main chamber, about 0.5 m above floor level) was identified by M. R. Domurad as belonging to a woman 20–30 years old (other bones remain to be identified). Some 30 to 40 pottery vessels of seven broad types

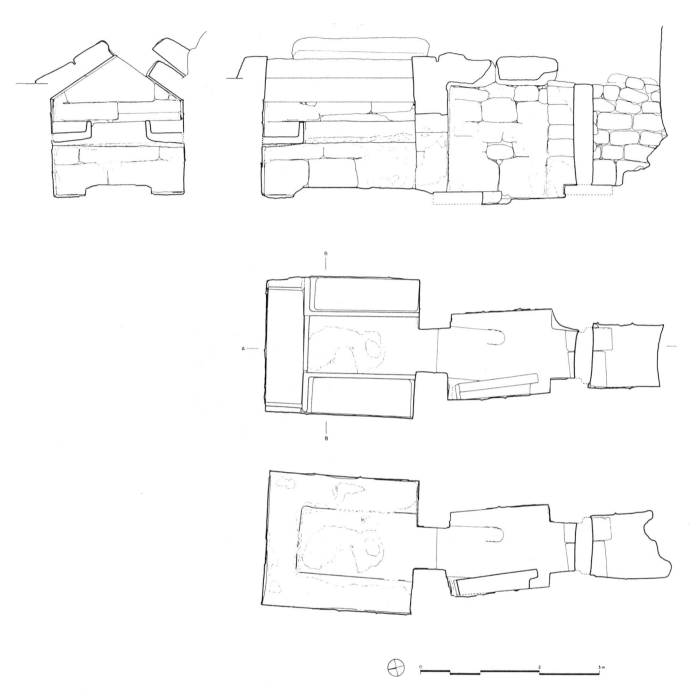

Fig. 28. Haci Oğlan, Tomb 89.11: plans, at floor level (bottom) and at level of stone benches (middle), and sections (top).

are represented in the pottery remains: four alabastra, two amphorae or similar closed vessels, eight narrow-necked small vessels, six to nine cups or bowls, one lagynoid vessel, three to four lekythoi; and seven to ten unguentaria. Three pottery lamps and one stone alabastron were also recovered.

Most of the diagnostic pottery and lamps appear to be types of the third and second centuries B.C.E.:

several echinus bowls and unguentaria, the lagynoid vessel, and a lamp of Broneer Type IX (fig. 29). Two pottery items of Archaic style were recovered from the tomb: a small skyphos fragment and a lekythos (body) of "Lydian/Samian" type (fig. 29).[32] The former is insignificant enough to be intrusive; the latter, relatively large and plain, is implausible as either an intrusion or an heirloom, but there is hardly another explanation. Given the disturbed context of the burial offerings, the predominantly Hellenistic styles of the ceramic material and the compatibility with a post-Archaic date of the pitched ceiling of the main chamber and other construction features suggest that Tomb 89.11 was built no earlier than the fourth century B.C.E. and was used in the third or second century B.C.E.

Sarcophagus Burials at Sardis

Higher ground southeast of Tomb 89.11 contained the ten sarcophagus burials excavated by the Manisa Museum (graves 89.1–10; figs. 30, 31). The following account is condensed from a report written by Manisa Museum curator Rafet Dinç and provided, together with the illustrations, by courtesy of the Manisa Museum director and staff.

The sarcophagi had been buried in the top of a hill or spur of the Necropolis massif, which before modern activity featured three small rises (tumuli?); they were exposed when the hilltop was bulldozed to make a flat surface for planting.[33] In general, the burials resemble those at Haci Oğlan excavated by the Expedition in 1961 (Hanfmann 1962: 30, fig. 25; 1983: 123). All ten sarcophagi have chests and lids of limestone. All the chests have the "Lydian bathtub"-type exterior form (bodies ovoid, rims rectangular in plan); two have ovoid cavities, the others rectangular cavities. Lids are double-pitched except for one, which appears to be a chest used as a lid. Both parts of that sarcophagus (89.10) have ovoid interiors and horizontally-faceted exteriors, like a sarcophagus chest in an early fifth century B.C.E. tomb excavated in the city cemetery by the Butler Expedition (Tomb 813; Greenewalt, Rautman, and Cahill 1987: 36–44).

Six of the burials had been violated, each by means of a hole created in the side of the chest (the holes are indicated by cross-hatching in fig. 30). Violation of the sarcophagi ranged from thorough (89.3 and 89.7 contained no bones or grave offerings) to partial, with eight gold diadems surviving in one (89.2). A seventh sarcophagus was half-destroyed in modern times, but until then may have survived intact (as suggested by the articulated condition of skeletal contents; 89.10). The other three burials survived intact (89.1, 4, 8). One of the three contained two skeletons, each of the others had one skeleton. Bodies had been placed in extended positions; their orientation, like that of the sarcophagi, is irregular (heads at both east and west ends in

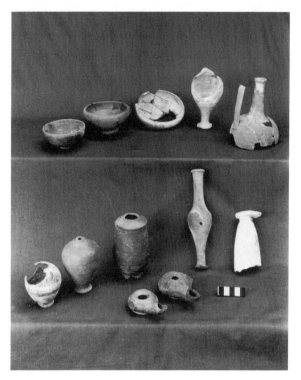

Fig. 29. Ceramic material from Tomb 89.11.

89.1; at the south end in 89.2; at the north end in 89.8), unless it was influenced by the deceased's age and sex, which have not been determined.

Most of the offerings are associated with sustenance and personal adornment, as is typical of offerings recovered from graves in the city cemetery.[34] The purpose of iron nails (one in 89.1; two in 89.2) is unknown.[35] Pottery and stone oil or perfume containers (lekythoi, unguentaria, alabastra) are common in other graves at Sardis. The more valuable offerings included gold diadems (the eight from 89.2, all made of thin gold and decorated with floral motifs in impressed dots); and silver phiale (89.8; fig. 31); a bronze bowl with spool lugs (in fragments; 89.2); and a bronze jug (89.8; fig. 31). Bronze mirrors were associated with three burials (89.3, 4, 7).[36] Offerings had been placed outside as well as inside the sarcophagi.

The three intact burials contained offerings as follows:

89.1 (with two interments). Four stone alabastra, one iron nail, two bronze fragments (one part of a button?), one bronze coin of Ephesos.

89.4. Four stone alabastra, one bronze mirror.

89.8. Two stone alabastra, one bronze jug, one silver phiale (fig. 31).

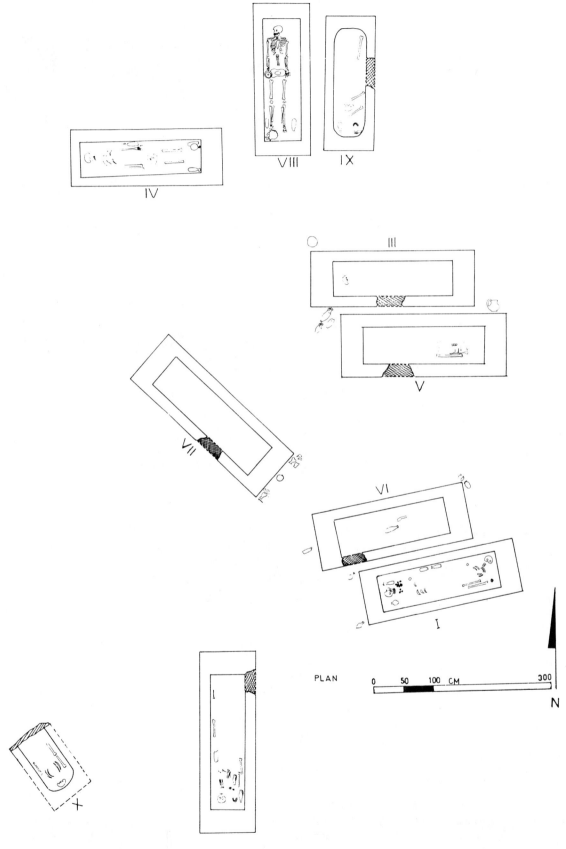

Fig. 30. Haci Oğlan, Sarcophagus burials 89.1–10, plan (with distances between sarcophagi compressed).

The placement of some offerings has a specific relationship to the sarcophagus or interment or both.
In at least three burials, outside offerings are at the
corners (89.1, 5, 7; also 89.6 ?); those offerings
were pottery containers for oil or perfume (lekythoi, unguentaria). Within 89.4 and 89.8 a stone
alabastron was placed near each foot of the interment, one in each corner (in 89.4 tilted upright, the
one by the left foot supporting a bronze mirror; in
89.8 resting on their sides, the one by the right foot
near a bronze jug). In 89.4 a stone alabastron rested
parallel to each forearm, between the arm and the
side of the sarcophagus. In 89.8 a silver phiale
rested near (originally in?) the right hand.[37] In 89.1,
29 gilded and pierced clay beads rested in the location of the neck or breast of one interment (with
head at the west end of the sarcophagus).

The ten sarcophagus burials may have a chronological range of two centuries or more. The bronze
coin of Ephesos in 89.1 is an issue of the third or
second century B.C.E., a date consistent with the
three unguentaria from the same burial. The bronze
jug in 89.8 (fig. 31) has a close parallel from Sardis that has been assigned a date in the fifth century B.C.E. (Waldbaum 1983: 149 no. 977), and the
bowl with the spool lugs from 89.2 probably antedates the Hellenistic period.

Graves at Bin Tepe

Two graves at Bin Tepe were excavated by the
Manisa Museum; the following information was
provided by director Hasan Dedeoğlu and curator
Rafet Dinç.

An Archaic sarcophagus burial contained several
complete items, including a bronze mirror with en-
graved "Aeolic capital" motif and a faience amulet
in the form of an eye of Horus (similar to examples
recovered from graves at Sardis; see Butler 1922:
118, ill. 124; Greenewalt, Cahill, and Rautman
1987: 49, n. 36).

An Archaic tumulus tomb (located between
Karnıyarık Tepe and Kır Mutaf Tepe, see Hanfmann 1964: 54 fig. 34), with dromos and single
chamber containing a carved and painted stone
kline, had been robbed; but remains of a wheeled
vehicle, which had been disassembled at the time
of the burial, were recovered in the dromos. The
remains included two short iron pins with bronze
ram-head terminals, two iron linch pins with
bronze terminals in the form of human torsos, two
bells, and two wheels that had been placed one on

Fig. 31. Silver phiale and bronze jug from Haci Oğlan sarcophagus burial 89.8.

top of the other at the outer end of the dromos. The
wheels, each ca. 1.60 m in diameter, had iron
clamps, which evidently secured segments of the
wood wheels and which are familiar from Assyrian
representations of chariot wheels. It also had iron
"tires" fastened to the wood rim by closely-spaced
iron pins with relatively large round heads; these
also are familiar from representations of Assyrian
and Achaemenid Persian chariot wheels (see
Dedeoğlu 1991, with illustrations).[38]

UNEXCAVATED ANTIQUITIES

A marble block from the inscribed triglyph-
metope frieze of a Roman building and a Hellenistic cylindrical marble altar with relief decoration
were recovered from the city site in 1988.

The architectural block (NoEx88.3/IN88.5) was recovered southeast of the Acropolis, near foundations
of the Roman aqueduct (for which see Butler 1922:
35–36 and pl. 1). It preserves one triglyph and metope, with a wreath in the metope and inscriptions in
Greek (*Halieia* on the border above the metope and
hopli/tēn within the wreath) that record honors for
an armed contestant, *hoplitēs*, in the Halieia games
(P. Herrmann, personal communication).

The altar (NoEx88.2) was confiscated by gen-
darmerie from a house in the village of Sart Mah-
mut. Its relief decoration is delicately carved and
consists of a bucranium and garland chain with the
following motifs above the garland swags: a serpent
(rising from a coil), a helmet (of "Attic" type) and
cornucopia, and a thyrsos.

C.H.G.

NOTES

[1]Excavation and other projects were conducted by the Archaeological Exploration of Sardis, or Sardis Expedition, which is jointly sponsored by the Harvard University Art Museums, Cornell University, the American Schools of Oriental Research, and the Corning Museum of Glass. The project is supported financially by many corporate and individual donors. The conservation program is supported by a grant from the Samuel H. Kress Foundation. Study projects connected with publication of the results of field work before 1977 are supported by the National Endowment for the Humanities. Field work was authorized in 1988 by the General Directorate of Antiquities and Museums, in 1989 renamed Presidency for the Protection of Cultural and Natural Possessions, a division in 1988 of the Ministry of Culture and Tourism, in 1989 of the Ministry of Culture of the Republic of Turkey. Each field season took place during three summer months.

It is a pleasure to acknowledge fundamental permissions granted by the General Directorate/Presidency, and the encouragement and support of its officers: General Director Nurettin Yardımcı, Acting President Altan Akat, Deputy Director General/President Nimet Berkok, Excavations Department Chief Mehmet Yılmaz, and Excavations Branch Directors Mustafa Karahan and Çelik Topcu. Messrs. Topcu and Mehmet Eskioğlu offered sound advice and welcome reassurances during administrative difficulties in 1989. The Archaeological and Ethnographical Museum in Manisa also generously supported, assisted, and encouraged Expedition projects; the Expedition is particularly grateful to Director Hasan Dedeoğlu, Deputy Directors Fatma Bilgin and Mustafa Tümer, and curators İlhami Bilgin and Rafet Dinç. The Government representatives were İlhami Bilgin in 1988 and Emir Çapraz (assistant in the Museum of Anatolian Civilizations, Ankara) in 1989. The Kaymakam of Salihli, Fethi Büyükaksoy, several faculty members of the Aegean and Ninth of September Universities in Bornova, Erden Karaesmen of Metaş Metallurgy Factory, Izmir, and İsmail M. Bacak of Desa Boiler and Machine Industries, Izmir, generously provided invaluable expertise and services in the examination and analysis of the iron and bronze helmet fragments recovered in 1987.

Staff members for 1988 and 1989 were the following (for both seasons where no year is given): C. H. Greenewalt, Jr. (University of California at Berkeley; field director); Teoman Yalçınkaya (Yapıtek Firm, Izmir; administrative advisor and agent); A. Ramage (Cornell; associate director and specialist for sector HoB stratigraphy and pottery); K. J. Frazer (Egypt Exploration Society; manager, 1988); D. J. Pullen (Harvard; administrative officer, Sardis Office; specialist for computerization program, 1988); K. A. Martin (Harvard; administrative officer, Sardis Office, assistant manager, 1989); M. LiCalsi (New York University, Institute of Fine Arts, Conservation Center; senior conservator, 1988); J. F.

DeLaperouse (New York University, Institute of Fine Arts, Conservation Center; conservator, 1988, and senior conservator, 1989); C. Snow (Walters Art Gallery, Baltimore; conservator, 1988); J. A. Sherman (New York University, Institute of Fine Arts, Conservation Center; conservator, 1989); L. J. Majewski (New York University, Institute of Fine Arts, Conservation Center; advisory conservator, 1988); K. J. Severson (Daedalus, Inc., Boston; advisory conservator, 1989); C. Z. Ratté (Harvard; senior architect, 1988); J. O. Fischer (Harvard; architect, 1988); T. D. Thompson (Ball State University; architect, 1988, and senior architect, 1989); S. M. Hickey (Ball State University; architect, 1989); C. S. Alexander (Harvard; draftsman and excavator); M. Fink (Cornell; photographer, 1988); C. M. de Boucaud (Cornell; photographer, 1989); C. English (Cornell; recorder, 1988); R. T. Neer (Harvard; recorder and excavator, 1989); C. Ratté (University of California at Berkeley; senior archaeologist, 1988; assistant director and specialist for Lydian masonry, 1989); M. L. Rautman (University of Missouri-Columbia; archaeologist and specialist for Late Roman pottery); N. D. Cahill (University of California at Berkeley; archaeologist, 1988, and senior archaeologist, 1989); M. J. Rein (Harvard; archaeologist and numismatist); E. Schluntz (Harvard and University of California at Santa Barbara; archaeologist); M. Bennett (Harvard; archaeologist and epigraphical recorder, 1988); G. Umholtz (University of California at Berkeley; archaeologist and epigraphical recorder, 1989); P. Herrmann (University of Hamburg; specialist for Greek and Latin inscriptions, 1989); B. K. McLauchlin (San Francisco State University; specialist for Manisa Museum displays); F. K. Yegül (University of California at Santa Barbara; specialist for graphic recording of the Artemis Temple, 1988); N. H. Ramage (Ithaca College; specialist for sector PN pottery, 1988); A. Oliver, Jr. (National Endowment for the Arts, Washington; specialist for Hellenistic pottery, 1988); M. R. Domurad (Center for Nutrition Research, Boston; palaeozoologist, 1989); R. M. A. Nesbitt (British Institute of Archaeology, Ankara; palaebotanist); E. E. and J. W. Myers (Boston University; specialists for balloon photography). The considerable clerical work required by regulations of the Ministry of Labor and the Social Security Commission was done efficiently and cheerfully by C. Şentürk (Manisa Museum). To all these for patience, hard work, high professional standards, and team spirit, hearty and heartfelt thanks.

[2]Conservation efforts included, in addition to routine work, repair and consolidation of a stone balustrade segment from the forecourt of the Late Roman Synagogue; backing and treatment for display of a Late Roman mosaic paving from sector ByzFort (Greenewalt, Cahill, and Rautman 1987: 36 and figs. 22, 23; Greenewalt et al. 1990: 155); examination by x-radiography and microscopy at Desa and Metaş firms (above, see also n. 1) of the

iron and bronze helmet recovered from sector MMS in 1987 (Greenewalt 1990: 1–28; Greenewalt and Heywood 1992; and Greenewalt 1992); and restoration of two pottery vessels with orientalizing decoration, one a skyphos from sector PN (Hanfmann 1962: 23 and fig. 16), the other a boat-shaped vessel from sector MMS (fig. 20).

Balloon photography included coverage of the Artemis Temple, Sectors PN, HoB, and ByzFort, the Roman Bath-Gymnasium complex with sectors MMS, MMS/N, and MMS/S, artificial mounds 1–4 on the north side of the city site together with Building C, the theater and stadium complex. For graphic recording of the Artemis Temple, see Greenewalt 1990: 23 n. 5. With the encouragement and support of Manisa Museum Director Hasan Dedeoğlu and staff, displays of artifacts from Sardis together with graphic and photographic material and some labels in Turkish and English were installed in the Manisa Museum to illustrate the following subjects: crafts (rock crystal, bone and ivory, glass) and food preparation in Archaic Sardis; fine quality and unusual drinking vessels of the Archaic period; traditions about Croesus; cults of Sardis; and artifacts of the Late Roman Synagogue and Jewish community at Sardis. Greek and Latin inscriptions studied by Herrmann include several, the significance and nature of which had previously been missed. These included two monumental inscriptions, one a Greek and Latin bilingual honoring Tiberius, the other of Antonine date and inscribed on a wall revetment, presumably from the Bath-Gymnasium complex; and a modest-sized inscription reporting honors to the Sardian Polybios (identified by Herrmann with the dedicant in Buckler and Robinson 1932: 65 no. 45) from the Athenian Areopagus.

[3] For a thorough preliminary analysis of the MMS/N colonnade, see G. Umholtz, 1989 MMS/N Final Report manuscript.

[4] From nearby fill were recovered a marble votive block (S89.3/9683) and, according to the workmen, a marble table leg with panther head and leg (for the type, see Richter 1966: 111–12, figs. 572, 576). The upper surface of the votive block is carved with a central cockle shell and two flanking flat bosses; the front side is inscribed ΔΩΡΟΝ/ΜΓΑΤΜΑ: "gift; the third month, first day, year 341." According to P. Herrmann, whose reading is presented here, the date corresponds to 256/257 C.E. in the Sullan calendar.

[5] Clearly belonging to the street colonnade were several monolithic column shaft fragments of a friable green stone. A few had been shattered in antiquity and been repaired with clamps of iron embedded in lead.

[6] The latest coins recovered in both 1978 and 1989 date from the reign of Phocas (602–605 C.E., 1989.167; and 602–610 C.E., 1978.70, 1978.71, 1978.85, 1989.165).

[7] Several notable pieces of sculpture, recovered from mixed fill in the area, include a small nude male torso of Polykleitan style (S88.3/9591); a small draped female figure combined with a pier (S88.2/9580); and part of an Archaic anthemion (S88.5/9597), with alternating convex and concave petal centers (Ratté 1989: 253, fig. 176 [B20]).

[8] The *exedra* is well known among the Roman houses of north Africa; see Rebuffat, Hallier, and Marion 1970: 299–300, 317; Thébert 1987: 373–74. For the applicability of Vitruvian terminology in Late Roman times, see Hanoune 1984: 442.

[9] J. Nesbitt (personal communication) has pointed out that since such sealings were attached to letters, the object indicates only that a resident of the house was a correspondent of the deacon Kosmas. Crosses are carried by the wall paintings of Room II; for the water tank in Room X, see Rautman in Greenewalt, Rautman, and Cahill 1987: fig. 2.

[10] For a similar apsidal room transformed to industrial use in late antiquity see Argoud, Callot, and Helly 1980. The latest coins recovered from the apsidal room date from the reigns of Justinian I (527–565 C.E., 1989.81); Justin II (567/568 C.E., C89.15; 572/573 C.E., 1989.89), and Heraclius (612–613 C.E., 1983.149). Among the objects recovered from the apsidal room was a small terracotta bulla (T89.12/9711). The obverse presents a bearded and laureate head facing right, with a circumscribed text, . . . TANTO . . . ; the reverse bears the impression of papyrus or similarly textured material. Concerning the general use of such clay bullae in the Hellenistic and Roman periods, see McDowell 1936: 1–24. J. Nesbitt (personal communication) has suggested that the bulla represents not an emperor but a government official or a private person; he has found the closest parallels in lead uniface sealings of the fifth and sixth centuries C.E., of which there is an example in the Dumbarton Oaks Collection (DO 47.2.1972).

[11] The earthwork of clayey earth also contained pottery of types earlier than "Achaemenid" bowls. Noteworthy items included a Corinthian fragment, P89.4/9625; a skyphos rim with Wild Goat decoration on the exterior and unusual vertical streaky glaze on the interior, P89.8/9631; a fragment with orientalizing figural decoration, P89.15/9642; and an intact miniature marbled lekythos, P89.17/9645. The earthwork "contained a significant number of earlier shapes and fabrics not represented in the mid-sixth century destruction debris of the Lydian houses (i.e., residential complex on the east side of Colossal Lydian Structure, text, below): grayware, bichrome plates, triangular-rim hydrias, early bichromes and black-on-reds, an omphalos bowl, etc. This suggests that some of the clay was dug from another area and redeposited here, together with its early material" (N. D. Cahill, 1989 MMS-III Final Report manuscript, 7).

[12] The beam socket is ca. 0.15 m high and 0.25 m deep; at the time of excavation it contained slight remains of carbonized wood. For such beams in Phrygian architecture, see Young 1960: 6–7.

[13] For Bronze Age fortification earthworks, see Parr 1968; Wright 1969. For mines, countermines, and protective glacis in siege warfare of later antiquity, see Greenewalt and Heywood 1992: 22, n. 3; Greenewalt 1992: 254 n. 13. For the date of the Persian capture of Sardis, see Cargill 1977; Burstein 1984.

[14] Between the clayey earthwork and the stony stratum was a "slight fill of sandy soil," from which were recovered fragments of "Achaemenid" bowls (fragments of such bowls were also recovered from the clayey earthwork); between the stony stratum and Brick Fall was a "thin layer of bricky earth" (N. D. Cahill, 1989 MMS-III Final Report manuscript, 8–9). The stony layer yielded more fragments of an orientalizing hydria, of which other fragments had been recovered in 1987 (P87.100/9523; with concentric circles on cream slip). From the "thin layer of bricky earth" was recovered part of a lamp with open central socket and open rim (L89.15/9713; similar to Broneer 1930: Type I, nos. 6, 7, etc.; Akurgal 1983: pl. 123, lower right).

[15] "The layer . . . contains a much higher proportion of red bricks than on the east—between 50% and 70%—and many fewer green bricks" (N. D. Cahill, 1988 MMS III-A Final Report manuscript, 8). "The upper levels of Brick Fall contained distinctly more red and more crushed brick, while about half a meter above the floor there was a higher proportion of green and brown" (Cahill, 1989 MMS III Final Report manuscript, 10).

[16] For Brick Fall on the east side of the Structure and for diagnostic pottery associated with it (two complete Attic cups—a Komast cup and a Little Master skyphos; one complete and one fragmentary Corinthian aryballos; and fragments of an Attic or Ionian Little Master cup and a Fikellura amphora) and C[14] evidence for a date in the mid sixth century B.C.E., see Cahill in Greenewalt, Cahill, and Rautman 1987: 22–24, 28–31; Cahill in Greenewalt, Rautman, and Cahill 1987: 68; Ramage 1986; Greenewalt et al. 1985: 73, fig. 22. For Brick Fall further to the north, immediately west of "Lydian West Wall" in sector MMS/N, Greenewalt, Sterud, and Belknap 1982: 20. For Brick Fall farther south, outside a south-facing wall in sector MMS/S, and associated fragments of an Attic black-figure closed vessel assigned by G. Bakır to the manner of Sophilos, see Greenewalt et al. 1985: 78; Greenewalt, Rautman, and Meriç 1986: 9.

[17] "After the settling and sliding of the rubble over time, the bones of the legs would have toppled and slid downhill. It is common even within the relatively protected confines of a tomb for bones to shift substantially. This idea is not entirely satisfactory, however, since some of the bones of the legs were not randomly displaced, but remained in clear, relatively natural orientation. The bones of the feet were still articulated. This theory then requires that sufficient decomposition took place such that the legs relaxed from the hips while the tendons of the feet were still firm. This is not impossible, given the relatively greater number of ligaments there" (M. R. Domurad, 1989 Human Bones Report manuscript, 5).

Bones of the lower right arm and hand, together with debris between bones, were lifted in 1988 and cleaned in 1989 by Domurad. Because of the relationship of the stone to the thumb and last three finger bones, and because the stone was somewhat larger than most of the

pebbles that occur in Brick Fall, Domurad concluded that the stone was a selected artifact and that its presence in the hand was not fortuitous.

[18] Quotations are from Domurad's 1989 manuscript report (at Harvard Expedition headquarters, Harvard University), which contains considerable additional information and bibliographical references. See also Greenewalt and Heywood 1992: 3–5, 22, n. 9; Greenewalt 1992: 257, 260, and nn. 17, 19, 21.

[19] The only artifact recovered with the skeleton was a coin-sized metal disk, possibly silver, which rested near the east side of the skull (M88.12/9609).

[20] "Injuries at or near the time of death were also evident. The left radius and ulna each sustained two parry fractures. The fracture pattern was the result of warding off a very forceful blow, and no healing was evident. There was also a possible stab wound in the right seventh rib near the articular area (near the spine), but it was not entirely clear that this injury and occurred antemortem" (M. R. Domurad, 1989 Human Bones Report manuscript, 4; footnotes and bibliographical references omitted). See also Greenewalt 1992: 260 n. 19.

[21] The remains of wood items were separated by a vertical distance of ca. 0.30 m. One, ca. 0.01–0.02 m thick, was traced in a straight line for 1.14 m (i.e., about half the length of a spear; Snodgrass 1967: 38). The other was 0.05 m wide (thickness not determined) and traced in a straight line for 0.50 m.

[22] The only pottery item was a trefoil-mouth oinochoe of ordinary type (P89.66/9709), which rested against the back wall of the recess, near the southeast corner (shown in fig. 18); for the type (with dark glaze covering upper parts), see Greenewalt 1978: 13–15. The only other items recovered from the recess floor were two pointed iron objects (resting near the south wall) and "a curved bone strip, perhaps an inlay" (near the center of the recess; N. D. Cahill, 1989 MMS-III Final Report manuscript, 15).

[23] For substantial Roman architecture and deposits in this hill, see Greenewalt et al. 1983: 8 (part of a tile-floored room behind the south wall of the Roman street); Hanfmann 1965: 14–17 ("middle terrace west" and "middle terrace east"); Hanfmann 1960: 19–20 ("upper terrace").

[24] The test trench was prompted by the claim of architect T. M. Wilkinson in 1983, during the setting of an architectural marker, that mudbrick had been exposed there.

[25] The salvage excavation took place underneath the foundations of a Late Roman wall (the north-south wall that separates spaces III-VI and IV of the Late Roman residential complex; fig. 5), which creates the eastern limit of 1984–1986 excavations in the Lydian stratum, and which was becoming undermined as a result of erosion of ancient debris underneath it during the winter of 1988–1989. A relatively large quantity of pottery fragments and nine pyramidal loomweights were recovered; most of that material evidently came from the floor of the yard zone or pit in front of the kitchen space (cf. Cahill in Greenewalt et al. 1990: 143–55).

The boat-shaped vessel with orientalizing decoration (P86.15/9223) was restored with the missing terminal facing inward, an orientation that seemed to the writer more plausible than the—literally ship-like—outward-facing orientation suggested in Greenewalt *et al.* 1990: 152. The tip of the spout (fig. 20) was recovered in 1989, among scraps that had been saved in 1986. For the orientalizing decoration, see the 1988 drawing by C. S. Alexander (Greenewalt 1989: 277 fig. 12). Pottery items repaired and inventoried in 1989 included two lydions (P89.18/9646, P89.20/9648) and two skyphoi (P89.19/9647, P89.21/9649).

[26]"Most bones from the left side of the skeleton, with the exception of the skull, were represented, including: most of the thoracic and lumbar vertebrae with associated ribs, fragments of the humerus, radius and ulna, most of the hand (some still articulated), both innominates, the femur, and parts of the foot and ankle.... Preservation was moderately good, aided by application, of a water-soluble PVA mixture at the time of excavation. With the exception of phalanges, metatarsals, and metacarpals, no bones were complete" (M. R. Domurad, 1989 Human Bones Report manuscript, 6).

[27]"The most common diagnostic pottery shape ... is a local Asia Minor variant of the Late Roman C shallow dish with rouletted rim" (M. J. Rein, 1989 Sardis East Byzantine Fortress Trench 16 Final Report manuscript, 4). Excavator Rein supplies a reference to Hayes 1972: 408–10. Six of 45 coins were legible; the earliest is of Constantius II (337–361 C.E.; C89.5), the latest of Honorius (394–423 C.E.; C89.6). The identifications are by Rein. Of the few post-antique artifacts recovered from the trench, by far the most noteworthy is a fragmentary silver coin of the Aydinid ruler Isa Beg (1348–1404 C.E.; cf. Bates, in Buttrey *et al.* 1981: 241 no. 47). The identification is by İ. Bilgin.

[28]Good examples of Archaic or Classical sandstone masonry in and around Sardis include walls at sectors AcN (Hanfmann 1961: 37–39) and MMS/N (Greenewalt, Cahill, and Rautman 1987: 31–33), and a group of three tumulus tomb chambers near the village of Alahıdır, west of Sardis (McLauchlin 1985: 257–59).

[29]The walls of the tomb chamber in the tumulus of Alyattes, and of at least one other tomb chamber in a tumulus at Bin Tepe (discovered by N. D. Cahill and the writer in the summer of 1989), are of marble. For the tumulus of Alyattes chamber, see Greenewalt *et al.* 1983: 26–27 and references; for that chamber and for materials and techniques of Archaic masonry construction at Sardis in general, see Ratté 1989.

[30]The chamber tomb was located in a vineyard owned by Osman Dursun. Design and construction are characteristic of tumulus tombs, and the irregular, un-finished exteriors of the stones show that the outside of the structure was meant to be concealed. The dromos faces uphill in the present gently sloping terrain, but surface contours in the immediate locale may have been somewhat different in antiquity.

[31]For the design and construction of tumulus tombs and rock-cut chamber tombs at Sardis and elsewhere in Lydia, see McLauchlin 1985; Ratté 1989. For tumulus tombs with double-pitched ceilings, see McLauchlin 1985: 25, 80–81, 191–92, 268 (at Sardis and Selçikler).

[32]The diagnostic pottery included two fragmentary echinus bowls (P89.43/9677, P89.45/9680), for which cf. Edwards 1975: 29–32 (nos. 32, 33); four fragmentary unguentaria (including P89.37/9671, P89.44/9679), for which cf. Thompson 1934: 473; one fragmentary lagynoid vessel with round shoulder (P89.50/9690), for which cf. Thompson 1934: 450–51 (D 30); and the fragmentary lamp of Broneer Type IX (L89.9/9670), for which cf. Thompson 1934: 388 (D 61), Schäfer 1968: 125–26 (K 3). Comparanda were identified by excavator R. T. Neer. The fragmentary Archaic skyphos and lekythos are, respectively, P89.35/9668 and P89.38/9672.

[33]Dinç reports that the sarcophagi are ca. 750 m south of the Ankara-Izmir highway and 467 m west of the Pactolus stream; and as plot no. 450 (in the name of Hatice Bilun Komuksu), section 24 of the Salihli Registry of Deeds. Their depth below modern ground level is not recorded.

[34]For Archaic grave offerings at Sardis, see Butler 1992; Greenewalt 1972. Armament was uncommon in graves. The Butler Expedition excavated more than 1,100 graves; the majority have no recorded contents, and many contained Hellenistic and Roman assemblages. Only six weapons are reported (four iron spearheads, one iron arrowhead, and one iron sword; from grave nos. 50, 231, 811, 722, 825) in the inventory ledger of H. W. Bell.

[35]One iron nail is reported from a grave (no. 143) with Hellenistic material excavated by the Butler Expedition, in the inventory ledger of H. W. Bell. For nails in Greek graves, see Kurtz and Boardman 1971: 216–17.

[36]There are 31 mirrors of bronze, silver, and iron from 26 graves excavated by the Butler Expedition, in the inventory ledger of H. W. Bell; for one of the silver mirrors, see Oliver 1971.

[37]Although silver phialai have been recovered from many graves in Lydia and elsewhere, the precise context is seldom recorded. For an exception, from Susa, see de Morgan 1905: 41–42, 43, pl. 2. For silver phialai from Sardis, see Waldbaum 1983: 146, 149 (three examples); see von Bothmer 1984: 22, cf. 24–28.

[38]For funeral carts, see, in addition to the references cited in Dedeoğlu 1991, Fleischer 1983: 45–50; Kohler 1980: 69; Karageorghis 1967: 22; 1973: 60–86.

BIBLIOGRAPHY

Akurgal, E.
1983 *Alt-Smyrna I, Wohnschichten und Athenatempel.* Türk Tarih Kurumu Yayınları, V.40. Ankara: Türk Tarih Kurumu.

Argoud, A., Callot, O., and Helly, B.
1980 *Salamine de Chypre XI. Une résidence byzantine "l'Huilerie."* Paris: Boccard.

von Bothmer, D.
1984 *A Greek and Roman Treasury.* The Metropolitan Museum of Art Bulletin 42.1. New York: Metropolitan Museum of Art.

Broneer, O.
1930 *Terracotta Lamps. Corinth IV, Part 2.* Cambridge, MA: Harvard.

Buckler, W. H.., and Robinson, D. M.
1932 *Sardis VII, Greek and Latin Inscriptions.* Leiden: Brill.

Burstein, S. M.
1984 A New *Tabula Iliaca*: The Vasek Polak Chronicle. *J. P. Getty Museum Journal* 12: 153–62.

Butler, H. C.
1922 *Sardis I, the Excavations Part 1, 1910–1914.* Leiden: Brill.

Buttrey, T. V.; Johnston, A.; MacKenzie, K. M.; and Bates, M. L.
1981 *Greek, Roman, and Islamic Coins from Sardis.* Sardis Monograph 7. Cambridge, MA: Harvard University.

Cargill, J.
1977 The Nabonidus Chronicle and the Fall of Lydia. *American Journal of Ancient History* 2: 97–116.

Dedeoğlu, H.
1991 Lydia'da Bir Tumulus Kazısı. Pp. 119–49 in *I. Müze Kurtarma Kazıları Semineri.* Ankara: T. C. Kültür Bakanlığı, Anıtlar ve Müzeler Genel Müdürlüğü.

Edwards, G. R.
1975 *Corinthian Hellenistic Pottery. Corinth VII, Part 3.* Princeton: American School of Classical Studies at Athens.

Fleischer, R.
1983 *Der Klagefrauensarkophag aus Sidon.* Istanbuler Forschungen 34. Tübingen: Wasmuth.

Greenewalt, C. H., Jr.
1972 Two Lydian Graves at Sardis. *California Studies in Classical Antiquity* 5: 113–45.

1978 *Ritual Dinners in Early Historic Sardis.* University of California Publications: Classical Studies 17. Berkeley: University of California.

1979 The Sardis Campaign of 1977. *Bulletin of the American Schools of Oriental Research* 233: 1–32.

1989 Excavation at Sardis, 1978–1988. *Türk Arkeoloji Dergisi* 28: 263–85.

1990 The Sardis Campaign of 1987. *Bulletin of the American Schools of Oriental Research Supplement* 27: 1–28.

1992 When a Mighty Empire was Destroyed: The Common Man at the Fall of Sardis, ca. 546 B.C. *Proceedings of the American Philosophical Society* 136: 247–71.

Greenewalt, C. H., Jr.; Cahill, N. D.; Dedeoğlu, H.; and Herrmann, P.
1990 The Sardis Campaign of 1986. *Bulletin of the American Schools of Oriental Research Supplement* 26: 137–77.

Greenewalt, C. H., Jr.; Cahill, N. D.; and Rautman, M. L.
1987 The Sardis Campaign of 1984. *Bulletin of the American Schools of Oriental Research Supplement* 25: 13–54.

Greenewalt, C. H., Jr., and Heywood, A. M.
1992 A Helmet of the Sixth Century B.C. from Sardis. *Bulletin of the American Schools of Oriental Research* 285: 1–31.

Greenewalt, C. H., Jr.; Ramage, A.; Sullivan, D. G.; Nayır, K.; and Tulga, A.
1983 The Sardis Campaigns of 1979 and 1980. *Bulletin of the American Schools of Oriental Research* 249: 1–44.

Greenewalt, C. H., Jr.; Rautman, M. L.; and Cahill, N. D.
1987 The Sardis Campaign of 1985. *Bulletin of the American Schools of Oriental Research Supplement* 25: 55–92.

Greenewalt, C. H., Jr.; Rautman, M. L.; and Meriç, R.
1986 The Sardis Campaign of 1983. *Bulletin of the American Schools of Oriental Research Supplement* 24: 1–30.

Greenewalt, C. H., Jr.; Sterud, E. L.; and Belknap, D. F.
1982 The Sardis Campaign of 1978. *Bulletin of the American Schools of Oriental Research* 245: 1–34.

Greenewalt, C. H., Jr.; Sullivan, D. G.; Ratté, C.; and Howe, T. N.
1985 The Sardis Campaigns of 1981 and 1982. *Bulletin of the American Schools of Oriental Research Supplement* 23: 53–92.

Hanfmann, G. M. A.
1960 Excavations at Sardis, 1959. *Bulletin of the American Schools of Oriental Research* 157: 8–43.

1961 The Third Campaign at Sardis (1960). *Bulletin of the American Schools of Oriental Research* 162: 8–49.

1962 The Fourth Campaign at Sardis (1961). *Bulletin of the American Schools of Oriental Research* 166: 1–57.

1964 The Sixth Campaign at Sardis (1963). *Bulletin of the American Schools of Oriental Research* 174: 3–58.

1965 The Seventh Campaign at Sardis (1964). *Bulletin of the American Schools of Oriental Research* 177: 2–37.

1983 *Sardis from Prehistoric to Roman Times; results of the Archaeological Exploration of Sardis 1958–1975.* Cambridge, MA: Harvard University.

Hanoune, R.
1984 La maison romaine: Nouveautés. Pp. 431–46 in *Apamée de Syrie. Bilan des recherches archéologiques 1973–1979, Aspects de l'architecture domestique d'Apamée*, ed. J. Balty. Fouilles d'Apamée de Syrie, Miscellanea 13. Brussels: Centre belge de recherches archéologiques à Apamée de Syrie.

Hayes, J. W.
1972 *Late Roman Pottery.* London: British School at Rome.

Karageorghis, V.
1967 *Excavations in the Necropolis of Salamis I.* Salamis III. Nicosia: Department of Antiquities of Cyprus.

1973 *Excavations in the Necropolis of Salamis III.* Salamis V. Nicosia: Department of Antiquities of Cyprus.

Kohler, E. L.
1980 Cremations of the Middle Phrygian Period at Gordion. Pp. 65–89 in *From Athens to Gordion: the Papers of a Memorial Symposium for Rodney S. Young*, ed. K. DeVries. University Museum Papers, 1. Philadelphia: University of Pennsylvania.

Kurtz, D., and Boardman, J.
1971 *Greek Burial Customs.* Aspects of Greek and Roman Life. London: Thames and Hudson.

Lawrence, A. W.
1979 *Greek Aims in Fortification.* Oxford: Clarendon.

McDowell, R. H.
1935 *Stamped and Inscribed Objects from Seleucia on the Tigris.* University of Michigan Humanistic Series 36. Ann Arbor: University of Michigan.

McLauchlin, B. K.
1985 Lydian Graves and Burial Customs. Unpublished Ph.D. Dissertation, University of California at Berkeley.

de Morgan, J.
1905 Découverte d'une Sépulture Achéménide à Suse. *Mémoires de la Délégation en Perse* 8: 29–58.

Nylander, C.
1970 *Ionians in Pasargadae; Studies in Old Persian Architecture.* Boreas; Uppsala Studies in Ancient Mediterranean and Near Eastern Civilizations 1. Uppsala: Uppsala University.

Oliver, A., Jr.
1971 A Bronze Mirror from Sardis. Pp. 113–20 in *Studies Presented to George M. A. Hanf-*

mann, eds. D. G. Mitten, J. G. Pedley, and J. A. Scott. Fogg Art Museum, Harvard University, Monographs in Art and Archeology 2. Cambridge, MA: Harvard.

Parr, P. J.
1968 The Origin of the Rampart Fortifications of Middle Bronze Age Palestine and Syria. *Zeitschrift des Deutschen Palästina-Vereins* 84: 18–45.

Payne, H.
1931 *Necrocorinthia: A study of Corinthian art in the Archaic period.* Oxford: Clarendon.

Ramage, N. H.
1986 Two New Attic Cups and the Siege of Sardis. *American Journal of Archaeology* 90: 419–24.

Ratté, C. J.
1989 *Lydian Masonry and Monumental Architecture at Sardis.* Unpublished Ph.D. Dissertation, University of California at Berkeley.

Rautman, M. L.
1990 Another Late Roman Well at Sardis. *American Journal of Archaeology* 94: 334.

Rebuffat, R.; Hallier, G.; and Marion, J.
1970 *Thamusida. Fouilles du service des antiquités du Maroc II.* Mélanges d'Archéologie et d'Histoire de l'École Française de Rome, Supplément 2. Rome: École Française de Rome.

Richter, G. M. A.
1966 *The Furniture of the Greeks, Etruscans and Romans.* London: Phaidon.

Schäfer, G.
1968 *Hellenistische Keramik aus Pergamon.* Pergamenische Forschungen 2. Berlin: de Gruyter.

Snodgrass, A. M.
1967 *Arms and Armour of the Greeks.* Aspects of Greek and Roman Life. London: Thames and Hudson.

Stronach, D. B.
1978 *Pasargadae; a Report on the Excavations Conducted by the British Institute of Persian Studies from 1961 to 1963.* Oxford: Clarendon.

Thompson, H. A.
1934 Two Centuries of Hellenistic Pottery. *Hesperia* 3: 311–480.

Waldbaum, J. C.
1983 *Metalwork from Sardis: The Finds Through 1974.* Sardis Monograph 8. Cambridge, MA: Harvard.

Wright, G. R. H.
1969 Iran and the Glacis. *Zeitschrift des Deutschen Palästina-Vereins* 85: 24–34.

Young, R. S.
1960 Gordion: Phrygian Construction and Architecture. *Expedition* 2: 2–9.

Underwater Explorations at Paphos, Cyprus: The 1991 Preliminary Survey

ROBERT L. HOHLFELDER
Department of History
University of Colorado
Boulder, CO 80309–0234

JOHN R. LEONARD
Department of Classics
University of Texas
Austin, TX 78712

The 1991 underwater explorations at Paphos, Cyprus, were designed to investigate the ancient harbor and associated installations that made the site a famous seaport in antiquity. The project had a certain urgency because development is rapidly obscuring early remains. This article summarizes the ancient literary descriptions, all previous archaeological investigations, and the preliminary results of the 1991 season. It concludes with suggestions for further exploration, should that prove possible.

INTRODUCTION

The ancient city of Nea Paphos (hereafter simply Paphos), so named to distinguish it from the nearby religious sanctuary of Aphrodite at Palaepaphos some 16 km to the southeast, lay along the coast of southwestern Cyprus (34°45′N, 32°24′E; fig. 1). It covered an area of more than 90 ha of relatively flat terrain that gradually rose from sea level (cf. Daszewski 1987: 174, who reported it at 90 ha and Nicolaou 1966: 567, whose estimate was 95 ha). Two hills command the site: the Pharos hill or the *Phanari*, the location of the modern lighthouse in the northwestern precinct; and the Fabrica at the northeastern end of the city. In antiquity, its hinterland was rich with forests of cedar, pine, and cypress and was endowed with numerous copper mines (Hauben 1987: 217).

The most important topographical feature from the perspective of the city's maritime history was a promontory that extended southwest from the coast (fig. 2). During the spring and summer, when ancient mariners preferred to sail and the prevailing winds off western Cyprus were from the northwest or west, this headland offered a reasonably sheltered natural anchorage in its lee (Mahoney 1988: 49; Casson 1971: 270). When it was first used as a roadstead is unknown, but the presence of a safe mooring and a readily accessible and strategically important supply of timber probably attracted the interest and ships of the great powers of the eastern Mediterranean long

before a harbor was constructed. Evidence of Mycenaean settlement, for example, has been found in the general area of Paphos, but not yet at the site itself (Nicolaou 1966: 562).

As a naturally favored anchorage along the western Cypriot littoral, Paphos was landfall for ships sailing east from Rhodes and points beyond en route to the Levant or Egypt. Owing to wind patterns and the counterclockwise currents that circle the island, Paphos's role in long distance seafaring was always more prominent for ships heading west to east and north to south. Shipping did occur in the reverse directions, but it was more difficult to sail into the prevailing winds.

Although Paphos offered both safe haven and easy access to vital natural resources from the very beginning of open-water sailing on the Mediterranean and even earlier for local coasting, it may have shared maritime importance before the Hellenistic Age with a natural roadstead that served neighboring Palaepaphos, an urban settlement whose origins are much earlier. Located near the traditional site of Aphrodite's birth from the sea, the older city featured a major temple to this goddess that attracted pilgrims from throughout the Mediterranean world. Its status was unchallenged until a city evolved at the Paphos late in the fourth century B.C. Only then would Palaepaphos's anchorage, located along what Mitford (1980: 1313) called an inhospitable coast, have been eclipsed by the superior maritime installations that developed concurrently with the founding of this new metropolis.

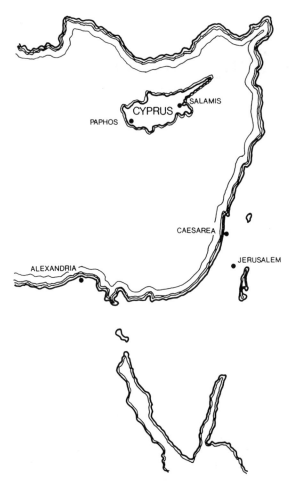

Fig. 1. Cyprus and the Eastern Mediterranean (K. H. Barth).

FOUNDING OF THE HARBOR AND RELEVANT ANCIENT TESTIMONIA

The traditional founder of Paphos was supposedly Agapenor, king of Tegea, who was blown off course during his *nostos* following the fall of Troy and reached Cyprus where he founded both Paphos and a temple of Aphrodite at Palaepaphos (Nicolaou 1966: 562 citing Strabo 14.6.3 and Pausanias 8.5.2). Recent scholarship, however, attributes the actual foundation to a local king named Nicocles sometime after 321/320 B.C.E., although the construction of the first true harbor at the site may have come slightly later (Nicolaou 1966: 564; Daszewski 1987: 171).

After 312 B.C.E. Ptolemy I became directly involved in the destiny of the port city (Mitford 1980: 1309; Daszewski 1987: 174). Sometime later, it appears that he assumed control of Nico-

cles's city and proceeded to enhance its installations on land and in the sea according to his own plans and needs. He clearly recognized the island's strategic position between the emerging kingdoms of the Diadochi, and the importance of local supplies of timber and copper; Cyprus was a stepping-stone to greater prominence for anyone who controlled it (Hauben 1987: 214). For Ptolemy in particular, the new port, with a large harbor facility positioned on the most direct north-south sea lane to Alexandria, was a valuable piece in the international chess game then being played in the balance-of-power politics of Alexander's successors. It would have figured prominently in his aspirations. Moreover, he had the resources to provide Paphos with facilities appropriate to its instant importance. Nicocles, on the other hand, may not have had the money or the reason to add to what nature had already provided his new city.

The estimated size of the ancient harbor, ca. 22 ha including areas now silted in and overbuilt with buildings, would have been too large for a kinglet like Nicocles and far more suited to the international plans and dreams of Ptolemy I (cf. Daszewski 1985: 280, who estimates its size as 22 ha or more; and Mitford 1980: 1312, who states that the city had a harbor "admittedly of not great size" obviously ignoring sections now covered with silt). It was, for example, as large as the great Outer Basin of King Herod's harbor at Caesarea Maritima, built c. 22–10/9 B.C.E. along the coast of ancient Palestine, an installation that also had been constructed with more than immediate and local economic needs in mind (Hohlfelder 1987: 1).

No archaeological evidence that can be clearly associated with this earliest harbor has yet been found, although the remains of the eastern breakwater that are still visible may date back that far (fig. 3). Even in the absence of specific data, it seems likely that Ptolemy's harbor would have been a *limen kleistos*, a closed harbor or one that could be closed (Lehmann-Hartleben 1923: 65–74; Blackman 1982: 194). Nothing less would have been consonant with the king's ambitions, or would have sufficed in that tumultuous age when the volatile geopolitical forces in the eastern Mediterranean had thrust Cyprus to the forefront of Hellenistic politics. A new city with a naturally protected harbor augmented by manmade installations, located near abundant and strategic natural resources, would have been a tempting prize for all the warlords of that age. Without fortifications to protect both its land and sea areas, it would have

Fig. 2. Paphos promontory looking W (Photograph, c. 1978, courtesy of the Department of Antiquities).

been a tempting and vulnerable target for naval assaults.

Evidence of land walls and towers dating from that period have been discovered (Nicolaou 1966: 572; Maier and Karageorghis 1984: 231). It may well be that those defensive structures were extended onto the two breakwaters as maritime fortifications. That could have been accomplished as part of the original building program of Nicocles or at a later date under Ptolemaic rule (Daszewski 1981: 329–30).

Ancient literary sources relating specifically to Paphos's harbor are scant and not very helpful.

Strabo, writing late in the first century B.C.E. (14.6.3), mentioned the existence of a harbor (*limen*) as opposed to an anchorage or *hormos*—a term he used with several prefix variations to distinguish roadsteads elsewhere on Cyprus that were not fully protected from the open sea, such as the one at Palaepaphos, which he designated a *hyphormos* (cf. Casson 1971: 362, who has a *hormos* as the anchorage within the *limen*; Strabo, on the other hand, makes a clear distinction between the two). The anonymous *Stadiasmos* or *Periplus Maris Magni*, perhaps written at about the same time, although its date is far from certain and may be as late as the fourth century C.E. (Pirazzoli *et al.* 1992: 375), mentioned that Paphos had a 'triple harbor safe in all winds a (297 = *panti anemo*). This elliptical reference probably speaks to a tripartite division of the anchorage enclosed by the breakwaters into three distinct basins, perhaps with each component having a specific function (here following Daszewski 1981: 332). Unfortunately, no other ancient writer, such as Flavius Josephus or Appian, who respectively described the harbors of Caesarea Maritima and Carthage in useful detail, wrote about this facility, so no literary explication of the *Stadiasmos* passage is available (*BJ* 1. 408–414 and *AJ* 15. 331–341; *Punica* 96).

Dio Cassius reported that after an earthquake in 15 B.C.E., the emperor gave monetary relief to Paphos and allowed the city to be called "Sebaste = Augusta" (54.23.7–8). The implication of his account is clear. There had been natural devastation beyond the ability of the Paphians to effect expeditious repairs. They must have requested and received imperial assistance to revitalize the port. In a calamity of such an implied magnitude, the two breakwaters that formed the harbor—both of which probably were constructed directly on the sandy ocean bed and thereby were prone to liquefaction—surely would have been casualties and may have required extensive rehabilitation to provide once again a safe haven in all winds. Furthermore, if the center of the earthquake had been offshore, tsunamis also may have ravaged this coastal city, particularly its maritime structures. One can safely assume significant damage to the harbor and associated installations.

Two late writers, Orosius and St. Jerome, offer additional information. The first recorded the tectonic destruction of the city in 77 C.E., a disaster from which it recovered (7.9.11). Around 390 C.E., Jerome commented on the ruinous state of the ancient city at that time (*Vita S. Hilaronis*, 42 = *PL*, col. 52). His text provides a literary confirmation of the calamitous results of the earthquake(s) of the fourth century that had struck the southwestern Cypriot coast with horrific impact. Devastation was not restricted to this port city (Soren and Lane 1981; 181, who discuss whether there was one or more earthquakes in the fourth century). Life throughout that section of Cyprus was severely disrupted. Curium, for example, was another victim (Jensen 1985: 307, who dates the earthquake to 21 July 365 C.E., following Ammianus Marcellinus 26.10.15–19.).

Paphos's harbor, however, appears never to have revived fully after the tectonic paroxysms of the

fourth century that culminated in 365 C.E. Perhaps partly in response to cumulative natural damage to its private and public buildings, the city lost its mantle of provincial leadership, and its port facilities probably retrenched accordingly. The political center of gravity of Cyprus shifted east again. The ancient capital of Salamis, renewed and renamed Constantia, became the new provincial capital and held that role throughout the island's Byzantine era (Megaw 11988: 139; Mitford 1980: 1321).

Although all of the above ancient references date from various chronological points in the Roman era, some earlier texts do survive that are potentially informative about Paphos's maritime life. Epigraphical evidence from Palaepaphos commemorated Pyrgoteles as a naval architect who built two large ships of the line for Ptolemy Philadelphus (284–245/6 B.C.E.). A painted graffito appears on a Hellenistic amphora found at Paphos, announcing that the vase had belonged to Pritios the Shipwright (Nicolaou 1966: 564, who discusses both texts). Both inscriptions imply the existence of a dockyard somewhere in the region before Roman times. Paphos was the most likely candidate. Perhaps one of the basins mentioned by *Stadiasmos* had served as such a facility in pre-Roman days (Daszewski 1966: 534).

No specific evidence for that type of naval installation at Paphos appears in later texts or the archaeological data uncovered to date, but a general observation by Ammianus Marcellinus, writing late in the fourth century C.E., may have applied to this port city before the earthquake devastation. He stated that Cyprus was able to build and fit a cargo ship utilizing only its own resources (14.8.14). The shipyard of Hellenistic Paphos could easily have survived through the centuries to meet the maritime needs of late Imperial Rome.

PREVIOUS OBSERVATIONS ON
THE PAPHOS HARBOR

Practically all archaeologists who have worked at Paphos have made some observations about the harbor, its history, and its configuration. In addition, numerous travelers to the site have commented on the state of the seaport of Paphos (Cobham 1908). Some of those accounts contain useful data regarding structural remains or topographical features no longer extant.

Hogarth, for example, commented after his visit in 1888 on the existence of a section of ancient breakwater faced with massive blocks clamped together with metal (Hogarth 1889: 7). No one since has been able to locate that structural feature, but his remarks often have been repeated (Nicolaou 1966: 578; Karageorghis 1968: 101; Daszewski 1981: 330). That type of construction, however, was not uncommon in ancient harbors. At Caesarea Maritima, a section of quay believed to date to the Herodian building program is still visible in what the excavators have called Area J. The metal clamps have disappeared, but their holes are still visible (Raban 1989: 144). Blocks with clampholes, however, were often reused in antiquity. At another location along the Caesarea coastline in Area S, it appears that an entire section of a dovetail clamped wall was lifted from its original site and relocated at some later point in the city's history (Raban 1989: 175).

Thus Hogarth's account, while consistent with what one might expect to find in a harbor dating to Hellenistic times, cannot now be verified. The blocks he described might have been original construction, or they could have represented reuse in a later period. The western breakwater (he calls it the northern one) has, however, changed too much in the last century to enable his observations to be confirmed or refuted today. Whatever Hogarth might have seen has either been removed or covered during one of the numerous renovations that have taken place since his visit.

From the 1960s on, several distinguished archaeologists have made useful observations on the ancient harbor, recounting details of the topography and structural remains that have since been lost to very recent development. Karageorghis noted in 1968 and repeated again in 1984 that one of the breakwaters (the eastern one) was 350 m long and that its western counterpart was 170 m (Karageorghis 1968: 101; Maier and Karageorghis 1984: 249). He also commented that the moles were constructed of huge limestone blocks, perhaps reflecting Hogarth on that point.

In 1966 Nicolaou prepared an invaluable comprehensive report on the physical remains of the ancient city and its topography, which has become the starting point for all subsequent studies on Paphos. He meticulously recorded many natural and manmade features of the site that have since been altered or disappeared. His sketch map of the site, including the line of the city walls and the breakwaters, has been replicated with minor changes in most subsequent treatments of the port city (Nicolaou 1966: 568).

Nicolaou was the first archaeologist to suggest that the modern topography of the site differs from that of the ancient harbor. In antiquity, the bay may have penetrated deeper into the promontory, greatly increasing the working area of the protected anchorage. In the central sector, it appears to have extended to the mound of a Byzantine structure known as Saranda Kolones (Nicolaou 1966: 567; fig. 3). Although he did not indicate the extent of the ancient bay on his sketch map, several subsequent studies have offered conjectures on its inland perimeter (cf. Maier and Karageorghis 1984: 227; Mlynarczyk 1985: 288; Megaw 1988: 137). He also noted that in the mid-1960s the eastern portion of the ancient harbor consisted of swampy ground.

Nicolaou also briefly discussed the first underwater survey of the harbor area and the surrounding coastline. That exploration was conducted between 1959 and 1961 by British military field engineers and sappers, both as an underwater training exercise and as an expedition to discover "the legendary lost harbor of Paphos." Their efforts, colorfully called "Operation Aphrodite I and II," have never been published, but their report has been cited as the source of a fanciful detail on the ancient harbor that appears in a popular Cypriot publication. Keshishian prepared a map of the Paphos area that shows a giant breakwater "a hundred yards thick" extending from the harbor to the Moulia Rocks some 4 km to the southeast (Keshishian 1961). He cited "Operation Aphrodite" as a source.

Although Nicolaou repeated that report of a mammoth breakwater, he rightly voiced skepticism as to its accuracy (Nicolaou 1966: 578, n. 44: "I cannot trace the origin of this tradition . . ."). He also noted that British survey had never claimed that such a mole had existed, although he does cite a relevant section from the report stating that the Moulia Rocks marked the "southernmost end of the great harbour."

To date, no scholar has attempted to confirm or refute what the British divers may have seen at the Moulia Rocks or to search for the massive breakwater whose existence is now embedded in local lore. All one can say is that a harbor formed by such a long breakwater would have been the largest ever built in antiquity; it would have exceeded any practical needs ancient Paphos would ever have had; and it would have been incredibly difficult and costly to maintain. Its existence seems most unlikely.

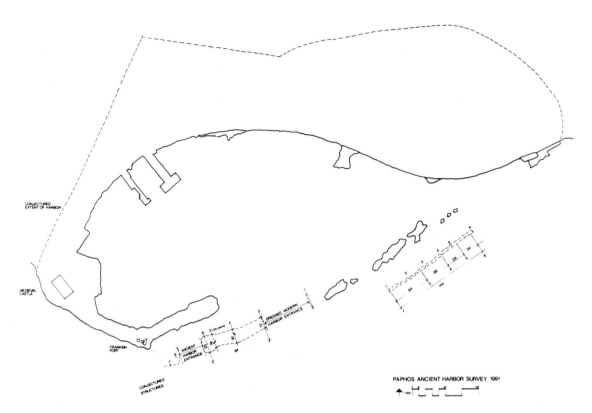

Fig. 3. The current official map of the modern Paphos harbor, upon which this one is based, does not show the most recent renovations to the western breakwater. The conjectured extent of the ancient harbor is based on Megaw 1988 (K. H. Barth).

Recent field work by Michaelides has added some important information to our understanding of the extent to which the bay of Paphos extended inland. In 1981, he found the remains of two sea walls in the eastern sector of the harbor. He dated the one farthest from the present shoreline (ca. 150 m) as Hellenistic in origin and the other one, closer to the sea by 10 m, as Roman. The most seaward structure may have dated from around the third century C.E. and may have been a renovation and hasty refortification of the harbor area. Geopolitical conditions in the eastern Mediterranean were then in flux, and Paphos's long period of security was threatened by attacks from the sea (Hill 1940: 243). In 1987, excavating behind the modern Customs House in the western sector of the harbor, Michaelides also found a section of sea wall and a large round tower that he dated to the Roman era—possibly as late as the third century C.E. (personal communication, 17 May 1991). Again, his discovery may offer testimony to the uncertainty of that century and to the city's growing concern for its safety.

Megaw also discussed both of Michaelides's finds and the delimitation of the inland sea wall. He offered his own version of a sketch map of the extent of the bay in ancient times (which is followed on fig. 3 here). He also noted a reduction in size of the total harbor in early Byzantine times to the western basin. In the seventh century, an area within the old city walls in that sector was fortified. It abutted what must have still been a viable anchorage in the lee of the promontory (Megaw 1988: 137, 144, 149).

Without doubt, however, the most valuable archaeological survey of the ancient harbor undertaken to date was by the Polish archaeologist W. A. Daszewski (Daszewski 1981). His underwater reconnaissance took place in 1965, before development had begun to revitalize what was then a sleepy fishing harbor that had changed little since the Middle Ages. Although no detailed plans, maps, or photographs were included in his account, his invaluable report will be the point of departure that all future marine archaeologists interested in the Paphos harbor will consult. Renova-

Fig. 4. Frankish Fort on the western breakwater. Traces of submerged spur are visible as well. Photograph, taken by the author while hanging from a parasail, looks N (R. L. Hohlfelder).

tions since 1965 may have given the harbor new life, but they have done so at the expense of obscuring much of its earlier history.

It may be useful to highlight some of Daszewski's observations, since his important article (in Polish) is not readily available to all scholars. He assigned the building of the ancient harbor to Ptolemy I, although construction may have started during the reign of Nicocles. Two artificial breakwaters defined it. In 1981, he stated that the western one was then 210 m long, but may have had an overall length of c. 270–280 m in antiquity. Its width ranged from 10 to 15 m. About 100 m from its southeastern *terminus*, a spur extended south from the main breakwater to provide additional protection to the entrance channel from westerly winds (figs. 3, 4). Where it branched from the main structure, there was a "huge defense tower" whose traces were still visible then.

Daszewski made no specific reference to the width of the entrance channel or to whether another defensive bastion stood on the *terminus* of the western breakwater. There is no sketch of that mole in his report, but his observations may have formed the basis for a very simple drawing of the ancient harbor, where a structure that fits his general description, is rendered in dotted lines. It appeared in an article written by another Polish scholar, J. Mlynarczyk (1985: 288, fig. 1).

In 1987, in a brief reference to his underwater survey more than 20 years before, Daszewski offered a different description of the western breakwater (Daszewski 1987: 174, n. 39). He stated there that this structure consisted of two parts—an east-west branch that stretched for ca. 235 m where it joined a second section that ran to the south (the spur he mentioned in 1981). He does not mention the breakwater extending farther than its visible length (either ca. 210 m in 1981 or ca. 235 m in 1987) or beyond the spur itself (cf. his 1981 report). The length of the spur was given as only ca. 50 m (cf. ca. 70 m in his earlier report). He reported the width of the breakwater to be only ca. 5–10 m, but in places as wide as 15 m (cf. 10–15 m in his earlier account). Again, he did not mention the width or location of the harbor mouth. His two accounts thus contain some significant discrepancies that are not easy to reconcile.

The eastern breakwater was longer, but narrower. According to Daszewski, its length at the time of the survey was 400 m, although originally it may have been 500 m or longer (cf. fig. 3). Its width, on the other hand, was only 5–10 m. A defensive installation, probably a fort, stood at its seaward *terminus*. There may also have been a second entrance passage to the harbor in its midsection, with traces of walls visible in 1965 inside the harbor near the opening. The breakwater was composed of cut blocks (2 × 0.05 m length and width) and had vertical walls even in its underwater portion.

Daszewski also commented on the *Stadiasmos* passage. He observed that the harbor was divided into three distinct sections: the westernmost basin would have been a military harbor; the central one

Fig. 5. The main mooring of the modern harbor with its flotilla of fishing boats and pleasure craft. Photograph taken from the roof of the Medieval Castle looking E (R. L. Hohlfelder).

was used for commercial traffic; and the eastern basin housed small fishing craft and the dockyard that had been active in the Ptolemaic period. But he observed further that it was possible that in addition to this divided harbor there may have been two other roadsteads. One would have been on the northwestern side of the Paphos promontory in a bay where the British recovered numerous artifacts during "Operation Aphrodite." The third would have been east-southeast of the eastern breakwater.

He concluded his report with observations on why the harbor fell into disuse. He suggested that tectonic activity was not a factor, but rather that damage to one of the breakwaters permitted the harbor to silt up so that it was no longer usable. Siltation may have accelerated after the fourth century earthquake(s) that destroyed Paphos; and it gradually grew worse over the centuries, increasing dramatically after similar cataclysms in 1160 and again in 1222.

THE 1991 UNDERWATER SURVEY

With Daszewski's observations as a starting point, the 1991 preliminary survey of the Paphos harbor area planned to study, map, and photograph any ancient structural remains before the rapidly developing modern harbor forever engulfs its more distant past. In addition, the survey team, consisting of seven members—two marine archaeologists, two architects, two students and one volunteer, hoped to identify locations where underwater exca-

vations might be profitably undertaken in the future. Possible anchorages beyond the harbor itself, including the Moulia Rocks area, were to be explored as time permitted.

Investigations began on 18 May and continued until 31 May. The season was planned to be short. Unfortunately, unusually high seas hampered our efforts. In all, only 49 hours of underwater investigation could be completed. The adverse sea conditions also prevented any diving beyond the immediate harbor area. All dives began and ended on shore or on one of the breakwaters.

Both of these structures were examined above and beneath the sea as fully as our restricted work schedule permitted. Ancient remains were marked with buoys for later location from shore (with theodolites), measured with tapes, and sketched by our architects (figs. 3, 9, 11). Points of archaeological interest also were photographed with a Nikonos V with a 20 mm lens. In addition, we used a jet-probing device to help determine sub-bottom profiles. That simple piece of equipment was developed by the Center for Maritime Studies of the University of Haifa for work on marine archaeological sites along the Israeli coast (Tuk-Kaspa 1989: 236–37). Compressed air is released from a tank through a long hose attached to a 2 or 3 m length of pipe (ca. 0.01 m in diameter). The jet of air emanating from its end penetrates the sand or mud of the ocean floor. It allows the pipe to descend for its full length or until a solid object is reached. One probe provides little information, but a series of them can determine a sub-bottom profile

Fig. 6. The modern western break-water with its exterior berm of large rocks and an irregularly shaped interior concrete quay. Ruins of the Frankish Fort are visible as well. Photograph taken from the roof of the Medieval Castle looking SE (R. L. Hohlfelder).

of an ancient structure or can ascertain the location of an entrance channel.

The techniques employed were very basic, but not inappropriate for this type of preliminary investigation. One of the realities of marine archaeology from its inception to the present has been the need to accomplish the task at hand with a minimum expenditure of funds, consistent with the required degree of disciplinary accuracy. The 1991 survey certainly did not violate this tradition.

RESULTS

The configuration of the ancient harbor now lies hidden beneath two millennia of human use and re-use. Natural despoliation has also taken its toll. Complete recovery of its original face or any later modifications in antiquity is impossible today. Even more of the ancient installations have been lost since 1965 when Daszewski undertook his survey.

The eastern breakwater appears not to have changed significantly, but the western one has assumed a new appearance. In the 1980s, it was enlarged significantly. Today's breakwater consists of two arms. One runs to east-southeast from the promontory; the other branches to the northeast at approximately the location of the Frankish Fort (fig. 3). Both arms have an external face of large rocks and an interior concrete quay, although the quay does not extend to the end of the northeast arm.

The east-southeast section is wider than its northeast counterpart, because the former element must bear the full attack of storm seas. Its exterior segment has an average width of ca. 22–24 m. A small retaining wall (ca. 0.85 m in height) contains this berm of stones and separates it from an interior concrete quay of irregular configuration and design (figs. 4–6). In most places the total width of the exterior rock segment and the interior quay is 52 m or more.

This current design has enabled a modern sea wall that had once adorned this breakwater to be removed. Its height was 4.5 m, according to Daszewski (fig. 2). The spoiling effect of the new exterior sloping face of rubble is sufficient to dissipate storm seas and safeguard the interior moorings without the additional protection afforded by this wall (fig. 6). By removing it, the port authority has not endangered the berths next to the concrete quay, and at the same time it has enhanced the tourist appeal of the site by opening photographic vistas for the many visitors.

Considerably narrower breakwaters in antiquity (ca. 5–15 m), however, would not have been sufficient to spoil incoming waves and assure a safe mooring unless they were surmounted by fairly high sea walls running down their spines. Without such wave-breaking structures, the harbor would not have been protected for all winds. Daszewski suggested that the ancient sea wall could not have been any lower than the one that existed in Paphos in 1965 (4.5 m). He was absolutely correct. It probably

Fig. 7. Courses of ashlars are visible in the lower seaward face of the Medieval Castle. Photograph looking N (R. L. Hohlfelder).

was higher; there may even be inferential evidence to that effect.

The Paphos Museum contains a stone relief, found locally, that features a personification of what might have been a harbor god. Behind that figure is a section of a seven-course wall surmounted with crenelations that might be the city wall or its extension onto one of the breakwaters. Its find-spot enhances the likelihood that the scene depicted might have been the harbor at Paphos.

Some of the blocks from such a sea wall may still be visible as building members in the two structures of medieval date that adorn the modern breakwater even today. The largest building, the so-called Medieval Castle (Nicolaou 1966: 567), is now in use as an occasional museum gallery and as a tourist viewing platform. The other one, the Frankish Fort (Megaw 1988: 141, fig. 2; figs. 3, 4 and 6 here), is in ruins and probably was the "defense tower" at the junction of main arm of the western breakwater and the spur that Daszewski mentioned.

Large ashlars are visible in both structures. A section of the Medieval Castle may have course of the blocks *in situ* in its lower exterior face (fig. 7). Whether or not that is the case, the largest blocks in both structures probably were not brought from great distances for reuse. If appropriate *spolia* existed on or near the breakwater itself, they most likely were used when both buildings were first erected. If this supposition is correct, and some of those large ashlars do date back to the original Hellenistic sea wall, their average size of ca. 2.5 ×

1 × 0.8 m permits an estimate of a height of ca. 5.6 m for a seven course sea wall, assuming that the relief in question does depict Paphos and is accurate in detail. In reality, however, even this considerable wall might not have been sufficient to deal with the worst winter storms.

Only a trace of Daszewski's spur running south from the western breakwater is visible today (figs. 3, 4). Its ruins were more apparent in 1965, but now they have been largely covered by the rock and rubble exterior face of the renovated breakwater. Since this jetty is now blocked from view, it may never be possible to know its date or original function with certainty.

East of the junction of the spur with the Frankish Fort, there appears to be a submerged structure that might actually mark the *terminus* of the western breakwater. Traces of what may be a vertical face of a wall were noticed there in 1991, but heavy seas prevented a closer examination (figs. 3, 4). If the breakwater did extend that far beyond the spur, it would give more credence to Daszewski's first description than to his second. If future survey and/or excavation does confirm the existence of a submerged structure here, its obvious function would have been to demarcate and guard the entrance channel it abuts.

The eastern breakwater, still in ruins because it is not needed by today's Paphian fishing boats, was always less critical to the operation of the ancient harbor, except during the winter, when winds were more likely to come from the south or southeast (Mahoney 1988: 49). In fact, its very existence

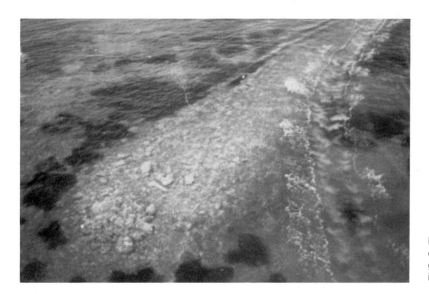

Fig. 8. The submerged *terminus* of the eastern breakwater. Photograph taken from a parasail looking N (R. L. Hohlfelder).

may have diminished the efficiency of the entire installation. Given prevailing winds and currents, water entering the ancient harbor mouth would have carried its seaborne sand clockwise from west to east around the enclosed anchorage. The eastern breakwater would have prevented that sand from returning to the open sea. Without channels cut through this structure to permit egress, siltation would have been an immediate and persistent problem in antiquity, as it is today. Water depths in the southeast section of the harbor are too shallow now for any practical purpose. A large part of what was the ancient harbor area has silted up or is useless even where water remains.

The preliminary survey of the full extent of the eastern breakwater challenges some of the data from the 1981 report. The overall length of the structure, ca. 600 m, appears to be much longer than previously suggested. The new estimate includes a submerged mound ca. 94 m long that extends southwest from the modern entrance channel (figs. 3, 8, 9). It may have escaped notice in previous surveys or may have been described as the continuation of the western breakwater beyond the spur in Daszewski's 1981 article. It was not mentioned specifically in his 1987 note, although he may have alluded to it. In that latter piece, he refined his earlier estimate of the eastern breakwater's length to ca. 480 m and noted that "the top is under water" (Daszewski 1987: 174, n. 39). That reference, however, is ambiguous. He could have meant this underwater mound, or he could simply have been referring to submerged portions of the eastern breakwater east of the modern harbor mouth.

The presence of a tower at the *terminus* of the eastern breakwater, immediately across the channel, was suggested by Daszewski in 1981, but its existence has not yet been confirmed (fig. 3). Architectural members are scattered about on the tip of the submerged mound. Two columns are particularly conspicuous features here; one is visible in fig. 8. The breakwater also was widest at this point (ca. 25 m), which may suggest that some commanding building may have stood there. For reasons mentioned above, a tower is a most likely prospect. Further investigation, however, is needed.

Less of this breakwater was visible in 1991 than in 1965. The second channel in its mid section (reported by Daszewski) was not readily apparent in 1991, although there is one breach that is a likely candidate (fig. 10).

Our investigations did locate a free-standing exterior sea wall made of rubble that ran parallel to the outer face of the eastern breakwater for ca. 144 m. Daszewski did not mention this structure, but it did appear in "Operation Aphrodite" photographs taken in 1959–1961 (kindly made available by the Department of Antiquities). Its width was ca. 2.5 to 5.5 m, with a height of -3.3 m below MSL at our buoy no. 6 to -4.15 below MSL at buoy no. 1 (figs. 3, 10, 11).

The wall's function and date are not yet clear. Even allowing for some sea level change since antiquity—perhaps as much as a 3 m eustatic rise in the last three millennia (see Stanley *et al.* 1992: 34

Fig. 9. Architect Chris Brandon sketching a column on the submerged *terminus* of the eastern breakwater (R. L. Hohlfelder).

and 47)—or some slumping due to earthquakes since the Hellenistic and Roman eras, it seems unlikely that the wall ever did more than reach the surface. Jet-probes at both ends of it tentatively indicated that it did not extend beyond its visible remains. It seems that it never paralleled the whole length of the eastern breakwater, but only a portion of it.

SOME THOUGHTS ON THE ANCIENT HARBOR

The renewal of Paphos in the last few years and the likely prospect of even more dramatic growth in the decades ahead diminish the chances of ever recovering more than the scantiest outline of the maritime life and history of the ancient harbor complex. Excavation beneath the sea may prove helpful, but there are limits to what now can be accomplished. Such field work will also be hazard-

ous, since boat traffic moving into and out of the modern marina is considerable and surely will only increase.

At this point, with the limited data available, few conclusive statements about the life and times of the ancient port can be formulated. It is possible, however, to offer some speculations about its harbor. They are offered as working hypotheses that will certainly be challenged and modified by future investigations.

It may well be that the building of the first major harbor at the site was associated with Ptolemy I (as discussed above, following Daszewski). Its early incarnation may have been as a *limen kleistos*, a harbor that could be both closed and defended against naval attacks. If it ever had that capability during the Hellenistic era, two towers, one on either side of the ancient entrance channel, would have constituted a normal defensive arrangement. One of the conjectured buildings probably would have served other purposes as well—perhaps as a lighthouse, a magazine for storing equipment for lifting the blocking chain, etc. Daszewski's "defense tower," apparently not at the *terminus* of the western breakwater, may have been a later structure or simply one of several towers that stood on the Hellenistic breakwater. The functions of towers may change, but their locations usually do not.

In antiquity, any large structures at the entrance probably would have served as navigational aids as well. The major navigational mark for this port was probably a large public building, either a temple or a lighthouse on the *Phanari*, the hill in the northwest quadrant of the city almost due north of the entrance (Mlynarczyk 1985: 289). When mariners spotted that monument from sea, a ship's captain could adjust his bearings to reach the promontory (fig. 12). He would then sight on the entrance towers and set course for the harbor on a northerly tack.

The maintenance of harbor fortifications against the ravages of the sea, and occasionally of man, was always an expensive and demanding proposition. Until Pompey had swept the eastern seas of pirates in 67 B.C.E. and Octavian had settled the fate of the Mediterranean world at Actium in 31 B.C.E., there would have been a need to attempt to maintain Paphos's harbor fortifications. But with the advent of a new era of peace and prosperity following those naval engagements, the military importance of Paphos would have faded, while its commercial role as international transhipment point would have grown.

Fig. 10. A submerged exterior sea wall parallels a section of the eastern breakwater. A breach that may have served as a flushing channel is visible in the upper l. corner. Photograph, taken from a parasail, looks to the NW (R. L. Hohlfelder).

After the earthquake of 15 B.C.E., the city revived with imperial help. We can reasonably assume that Agusutus's interest in Paphos guaranteed that any damage to the harbor facilities was repaired, at least to the point that the installations could meet the new imperatives of imperial Rome. Any military fortifications on the breakwater, dating from earlier times and now anachronistic in the *Pax Augusta*, probably were not restored (*contra* Blackman 1982: 194, who argues that fortified harbors were common in the Imperial era). The new order did not require a naval station there nor a closed harbor. What was important was to reestablish the structural integrity of the breakwaters, assuming that they had suffered damage in the disaster. It also may have been a time to implement modifications to improve the value of the harbor itself. It is likely that the Augustan harbor after its repair had a somewhat different appearance than its Hellenistic predecessor.

It is significant to remember the time of that disaster, 15 B.C.E. In that same year, Roman engineers dispatched from Italy by Augustus himself were nearing completion of their work at Caesarea Maritima (Hohlfelder 1992: 175). Although we cannot know who those master builders were, we are certainly in a position now to admire their genius in creating the first manmade harbor along a coastline of engineering impossibilities. Could Augustus have reassigned some of those engineers to Paphos to deal with harbor repairs there? His personal interest in the site makes that possibility very real. The emperor, of course, did not fund all harbor constructions throughout the Mediterranean. At Kenchreai (Greece), where another harbor was taking shape during his reign, there appears to have been no direct interest (Hohlfelder 1985: 84). But with Imperial involvement, as at Caesarea, everything was possible, including the importation of hundreds of tons of pozzolana and other building materials from the Bay of Naples and elsewhere (Oleson and Branton 1992: 58).

The spur, which guarded the harbor entrance by deflecting storms and currents, might bear the signature of those Roman engineers. Daszewski most recently claimed that it was one of two main components of the ancient breakwater, rather than an adjunct structure (Daszewski 1985: 174, n. 39). If the spur were actually the second arm of the western breakwater, the "defense tower" at its junction with the east-southeast arm would then have demarcated the western side of a very large entrance of more than 150 m (my estimate from his figures; Daszewski did not specifically address the issue of the channel's width or location). It would have been difficult to close such a wide mouth with a chain or boom. Wind-driven waves would have more easily entered the harbor through such an opening and disturbed the safety of the basin. *Portus* at Ostia may have required a 200 m entrance, but Paphos hardly needed such a large channel (Casson 1971: 368). It would have offered no advantages to outweigh the obvious disadvantages.

There is another possible explanation for the southern arm, if one assumes that Daszewski's first description of the western breakwater was more

Fig. 11. Architect Chris Brandon measuring the exterior sea wall. (R. L. Hohlfelder).

accurate and the total length of that barrier continued for some distance beyond where the spur jutted south (his 1981 estimate was ca. 100 m; fig. 3). In that case, the spur might not have been of Hellenistic origin, but it may have been a later addition to the main structure, perhaps added to correct a problem with the original harbor design. The entrance channel, as proposed on fig. 3, had a width of ca. 40 m. Its location was southwest of the modern harbor mouth, which appears to have been dredged through the eastern breakwater. It would have been wide enough to accommodate a large Roman merchantman or a Hellenistic warship with ease, yet narrow enough to permit closure with a chain when circumstances warranted.

Although much narrower than the harbor mouth that one can deduce from Daszewski's reports, it still may have been too vulnerable to seas and winds from the west and southwest. At some point, the spur may have been added to correct a design flaw. That occasion may have been in 15 B.C.E., when Roman harbor engineers, who were more advanced in harbor construction and technology than their Hellenistic predecessors, might have been called to Paphos as part of the Augustan relief efforts.

Elsewhere in the Roman Empire at about the same time, harbor engineers were attempting another experiment along the same lines. At Caesarea, two *pilae*-free-standing concrete structures built next to the entrance channel-served both as a foundation for colossal statues that distinguished the harbor mouth and as a final line of defense for

any south-southwest waves that had rolled around the Southern Breakwater (Oleson and Branton 1992: 56).

The Paphos spur may have been constructed with a similar intent—to repel both waves and sands from the harbor entrance when seas were running from the west or southwest. Its origin, of course, might have been before the Augustan era, but its probable purpose and design hint at a Roman engineering tradition.

There may also be an antecedent at Caesarea Maritima for the exterior eastern sea wall. The Paphos sea wall is very similar to a recently discovered structure in King Herod's harbor, which was constructed parallel to the great Southern Breakwater. That subsidiary wall, which also may have only reached or breached the sea, was intended to provide the first line of defense against winter storms that lashed the main structure at its most vulnerable point (Oleson 1989: 121).

Paphos's subsidiary eastern breakwater appears not to have served that purpose, but it may have been part of a novel experiment to deal with the continuous problem of harbor siltation. The engineers charged with repairs may have decided to create one or more outlets in the eastern breakwater to provide a way for water trapped within the harbor to reach the open sea before it deposited its sand. In other words, the opening that Daszewski mentioned might have been a flushing channel rather than another harbor entrance (cf. Blackman 1982: 199). Once again, a similar experiment to combat siltation had been implemented at Caesarea,

Fig. 12. The modern lighthouse stands above the ancient odeion. Photograph looks W across the agora (R. L. Hohlfelder).

but as an original design feature and not as a subsequent modification (Hoflfelder *et al.* 1983: 137).

Although a breach or breaches in Paphos's eastern breakwater could have been opened with little risk to the integrity of the harbor, the exterior sea wall may have been added to provide some protection for that channel from the rare, but not unknown, summer storms from the south or southeast. Waves coming from those directions would have lost most of their kinetic energy when they hit that outer wall, even if it did not reach the surface. At the same time, water from within the harbor could have flowed to the open sea, scouring the harbor clear of sand. Such a system would have been an ingenious attempt at a solution to a nagging problem. If it was implemented following the earthquake of 15 B.C.E., its basic concept might have been derived from a system that had just been implemented at Caesarea Maritima.

A similar opportunity for such renovations may have been presented after the 77 C.E. earthquake. Once again, if the emperors Vespasian and Titus had become directly involved in relief efforts, which is a distinct possibility (Maier and Karageorghis 1984: 250), engineers might have been sent from Italy to oversee repairs. The tradition of Roman harbor technology would even have been richer then, since the great harbor, *Portus* at Ostia, constructed during the reign of Claudius (41–54 C.E.), would have been recently completed (Meiggs 1960).

Without excavation, however, this scenario will remain only speculation. Even if the building of the spur breakwater and exterior sea wall were not related to either earthquake, they remain interesting structures that bespeak a considerable sophistication in harbor engineering. It will be important to try to establish precise dates of construction for both features. What is postulated here as derivative technology may turn out to have been original.

Daszewski's comment on the meaning of *Stadiasmos* also require some explication. His suggestion that the interior anchorage formed by the two artificial breakwaters was divided into three distinct basins is probably correct, although the defining jetties that separated them have not been located. Traces of those structures still may be visible jutting out in two places from the modern sea wail that supports the seaside road, but this observation is only conjecture.

Daszewski's assignment of specific functions to the three basins is also likely. Certainly the central one, with its proximity to the agora and the core of the city's public buildings, probably served as the harbor for international shipping into and out of the port city. A military function for the western section is probable at least in the Hellenistic period, since departing ships during spring and summer months usually would have had a favorable wind (west or northwest). The designer of the harbor must have anticipated occasions where a rapid deployment of naval vessels would have been necessary, and the western basin best afforded such an opportunity (Daszewski 1981: 334).

During the centuries of quiescence under Roman rule, the function of the western basin surely changed. Rome seems not to regularly have kept a fleet on the island, so a naval station at Paphos seems highly unlikely (Mitford 1980: 1345). As Blackman (1982) has noted, a major international harbor like Paphos may have had a distinct berthing area for ships and boats engaged in import-export traffic; as well as one for accommodating merchantmen laden with goods in transit. Such an arrangement would have facilitated general control and the collection of taxes and harbor fees. Ships sailing to Paphos as a final port-of-call presumably would have faced different assessments than vessels en route to some other ultimate destination (Blackman 1982: 194). Perhaps the former military station assumed one of those functions, while the central basin continued to serve in the other role.

If Hellenistic Paphos did have a shipyard, and the existence of such a facility is not yet certain,

Fig. 13. The ancient harbor may have reached inland approximately to the point where this photograph was taken. Photograph looks S–SE (R. L. Hohlfelder).

its location may have been in the eastern basin. If the Roman port maintained a similar installation, it probably was located where its predecessor had been.

Whether or not Paphos had two other harbors northwest and southeast of the promontory, as Daszewski suggested as one possible meaning of the *Stadiasmos* passage, is far less certain. Heavy storm seas (1+ m waves) and high winds (gusts of 20 knots) hit the port during the last two weeks of May, 1991. During such conditions, the bay northwest of the promontory would not have been usable as a landing station for ships or boats; so too the area outside the eastern breakwater.

Neither area was ever a harbor *per se*, but each surely played a role in the maritime life of Paphos. They were both secondary anchorages that could have been used when sea conditions permitted. Concentrations of artifacts visible in both areas (CyDive Ltd. staff—personal communication, May 1991) suggest such a role. It also was in the general area of the northwest bay that a statue of Aphrodite, now on display in the Paphos Museum, was recovered in 1956 (Nicolaou 1966: 596, fig. 26). Such fair-weather moorings were not uncommon for ancient port cities. Caesarea Maritima, for example, had several ancillary roadsteads to augment its main artificial harbor installation (Hohlfelder *et al.* 1983: 140).

When, and to what degree, the harbor at Paphos diminished in late antiquity cannot be ascertained from available data. There is no way at present to assess the damage from the fourth century earth-quakes, or to determine how quickly or extensively the maritime installations were repaired. When the provincial capital was moved to Constantia in the mid-fourth century, the financial burden of maintaining an elaborate harbor probably devolved to local authorities. It is possible that Paphos was unable to sustain all of its facilities. Gradual decline probably set in, as routine maintenance, so vital for any harbor past or present, was postponed. But even in a ruinous state, the ancient harbor basin would have been protected by the promontory and any remains of the breakwaters that had survived the earthquakes. It still would have served into the Byzantine era as the most important maritime installation on the western coast of the island. It seems, however, that by the Medieval period the maritime activities had constricted to the western basin. In particular, an earthquake in 1222 C.E. dealt the harbor a crushing blow—it simply "dried up" (Megaw 1988: 150, citing Oliver Scholasticus).

AGENDA

More fieldwork needs to be done at Paphos in the immediate future. Heavy seas aborted the 1991 survey before all of our objectives could be completed or our field data could be checked. A season of survey with an electronic theodolite and distomat will be required to confirm and complete all previous measurements. A thorough investigation of what remains of the spur and the possible structure at the *terminus* of the western breakwater adjacent to the entrance channel needs to be undertaken. A careful examination of the tip of the submerged mound of the eastern breakwater must also be carried out to search for any structural remains *in situ*. Another attempt to locate and confirm Daszewski's mid-channel in the eastern breakwater also must be made. The search for the exact line of the inland perimeter of the ancient harbor needs to continue, adding to the valuable work already accomplished by Michaelides (Karageorghis 1988: 855, citing a field report prepared by Michaelides; fig. 13 here).

Outside of the harbor itself, a thorough underwater reconnaissance of the northwestern bay and the area east of the eastern breakwater is needed. Both areas were surely ancient roadsteads. A record of their use in that capacity may still be recoverable. Finally, an attempt to locate the alleged ca. 4 km breakwater that extended to the Moulia Rocks

should be made, although the prospects for finding any significant structural remains seem remote.

Daszewski's pioneering exploration of 1965 began to unfold the secrets of Paphos's harbor. The brief investigation in 1991 added more data, but the preliminary survey is far from complete. When it is, all the working hypotheses advanced above and in earlier publications must be challenged by detailed, careful fieldwork. Only underwater excavations will enable scholars to move beyond speculations about the nature, date, and extent of the ancient maritime installations. Such a project will be challenging, since today's harbor is a busy one, and the danger to divers will be high. But it can and should be undertaken before more of the record of this important site is lost to the exigencies of the present.

ACKNOWLEDGMENTS

We begin by thanking A. Papageorghiou, Director of the Department of Antiquities when this survey was undertaken, for his endorsement of our efforts and for his positive encouragement. We are particularly grateful for his permission to use the dighouses at Paphos. Those accommodations afforded a splendid and intimate exposure to the beauty and magic of that very special site.

Others in the Cypriot archaeological community also generously shared their wisdom and vast knowledge of Paphos. In particular, we gratefully acknowledge the gracious and enthusiastic help of M. Loulloupis, D. Michaelides, A. H. S. Megaw, and V. Karageorghiş. Although our questions about a city they all know so well were often obvious, they had the patience to share their invaluable experience with us. They are all truly teachers as well as scholars.

At Paphos, the staff of CyDive, Ltd., particularly C. Dobbins, could not have been more helpful in meeting our diving needs and in sharing knowledge of the Paphos coast with us. Also, Police-Sergeant A. Nicolaous of the Harbor Police and T. Herodotou of the Paphos Museum helped our efforts in many ways.

While at Dumbarton Oaks in Washington, D.C. en route to Paphos, RLH benefited (as always) from discussions with Robert Browning about an island he knows so well. His love for Cyprus and its rich history is most certainly infectious.

We also are most grateful to S. Swiny, Director of the Cyprus American Archaeological Research Institute

(CAARI), for all his assistance and enthusiastic support. Thanks to his graciousness, RLH's introduction to the world of Cypriot archaeology could not have been more enjoyable or profitable.

Technical support for this survey came from Israel as well. We thank S. Breitstein, Chief of Diving Operations at the Center for Maritime Studies, the University of Haifa, for preparing a jet-probing device (which he helped develop with Y. Tur-Kaspa) for our use in Paphos.

T. Maslowski, Department of Classics, University of Colorado, prepared a translation of Professor Daszewski's 1981 article for us, as did E. Niesytto of the University of Texas, Austin. Their two translations were the *sine qua non* for this survey.

We extend our deepest thanks and appreciation to all of the individuals named above. With their support, this project has had an auspicious beginning.

In addition to the codirectors, our survey team consisted of C. Brandon (architect, London); K. H. Barth (architect, Boulder, CO); M. Nemechek (marine archaeological student, Hawaii); T. Thomas (marine archaeological student, Boulder, CO); and A. Sacoforas (businessman and diver, Cyprus). We wish to thank all of our colleagues for their enthusiastic commitment, hard work, and good cheer. There has never been a more dedicated and convivial band of marine archaeologists. In spite of some bad seas, our time together at that beautiful site was most memorable and productive.

BIBLIOGRAPHY

Blackman, D. J.
1982   Ancient Harbours in the Mediterranean. Part 2. *International Journal of Nautical Archaeology* 11/3: 185–211.

Casson, L.
1971   *Ships and Seamanship in the Ancient World* Princeton: Princeton University.

Cobham, C. D.
1908   *Excerpta Cypria. Materials for a History of Cyprus.* Cambridge: Cambridge University.

Daszewski, W. A.
1981   Port glòwny i przystanie pomocnicze w Nea Paphos w swietle obserwacji podwodnych. *Meander* 6: 327–36.
1985   Researches at Nea Paphos 1965–1984. Pp. 277–91 in *Archaeology in Cyprus 1960–1985*, ed. V. Karageorghis. Nicosia: Leventis Foundation.
1987   Nikokles and Ptolemy—Remarks on the Early History of Nea Paphos. *Report of the Department of Antiquities, Cyprus*: 171–75.

Hauben, H.
1987   Cyprus and the Ptolemaic Navy. *Report of the Department of Antiquities, Cyprus*: 213–26.

Hill, G.
1940   *A History of Cyprus, Vol. 1.* Cambridge: Cambridge University.

Hogarth, D. G.
1889   *Devia Cypria.* London: Frowde.

Hohlfelder, R. L.
1985   The Building of the Roman Harbor at Kenchreai: Old Technology in a New Era. Pp. 81–86 in *Harbour Archaeology*, ed. A. Raban. B.A.R. International Series 257, Oxford: British Archaeological Reports.
1987   The 1984 Explorations of the Ancient Harbors of Caesarea Maritima, Israel. *Bulletin of the American Schools of Oriental Research Supplement* 25: 1–12.
1992   The Changing Fortunes of Caesarea Maritima's Harbors in the Roman Era. Pp. 75–78 in *Caesarea Papers. Journal of Roman Archaeology* Supplementary Series Number 5, ed. R. L. Vann. Ann Arbor: Journal of Roman Archaeology.

Hohlfelder, R. L.; Oleson, J. P.; Raban, A.; Van, R. L.
1983   Sebastos: Herod's Harbor at Caesarea Maritima. *Biblical Archaeologist* 46.3: 133–43.

Jensen, R. C..
1985   The Kourion Earthquake: Some Possible Literary Evidence. *Report of the Department of Antiquities, Cyprus*: 307–11.

Karageorghis, V.
1968   *Cyprus.* Geneva: Nagel.
1988   Chronique des fouilles en Chypre, 1987. *Bulletin de Correspondance Hellènique* 112: 793–855.

Keshishian, K.
1961   *Romanic Cyprus.* Nicosia.

Lehmann-Hartleben, K.
1923   Die antiken Hafenanlagen des Mittelmeeres. *Klio* Beiheft 14. Wiesbaden: Klio.

Mahoney, P. J. B.
1988   *Mediterranean Pilot, Vol. V.* Taunton: Royal Navy.

Maier, F. G.; and Karageorghis, V.
1984   *Paphos: History and Archaeology.* Nicosia: Leventis Foundation.

Megaw, A. H. S.
1988   Reflections on Byzantine Paphos. Pp. 135–50 in *Kathegetria: Essays Presented to Joan Hussey for Her 80th Birthday.* Camberley: Porphyrogenitus.

Meiggs, R.
1960   *Roman Ostia*: Oxford University.

Mitford, T. B.
1980   Roman Cyprus. *Aufstieg und Niedergang der römischen Welt* 7.2: 1285–1384.

Mlynarczyk, J.
1985   Remarks on the Temple of Aphrodite Paphia in Nea Paphos in the Hellenistic Period. *Report of the Department of Antiquities, Cyprus*: 286–92.

Nicolaou, K.
1966   The Topography of Nea Paphos. Pp. 561–601 in *Mèlanges offerts á K. Michalowski*, ed. M-L Bernhard. Warsaw: Panstwowne Wydawnicto Naukowe.

Oleson, J. P.
1989   Area E. Subsidiary Breakwater. Pp. 120–24 in Raban 1989.

Oleson, J. P.; and Branton, G.
1992   The Technology of King Herod's Harbor. Pp. 49–67 in *Caesarea Papers. Journal of Roman Archaeology* Supplementary Series Number 5, ed. R. L. Vann. Ann Arbor: Journal of Roman Archaeology.

Pirazzoli, P. A.; Ausseil-Badie, J.; Giresse, P.; Hadjidaki, E.; Arnold, M.
1992   Historical Environmental Changes at Phalasarna Harbor, West Crete. *Geoarchaeology* 7/4: 371–92.

Raban, A.
1989   *The Harbours of Caesarea Maritima, Vol. 1: The Site and Excavations.* B. A. R. International Series, 491. Oxford: British Archaeological Reports.

Soren, D.; and Lane, E.
1985   New Ideas about the Destruction of Paphos. *Report of the Department of Antiquities, Cyprus*: 178–83.

Stanley, D. J.; Warne, A. G.; Davis, H. R.; Bernasconi, M. P.; Chen, Z.
1992   Nile Delta. *National Geographic Research & Exploration* 8/1: 22–51.

Tur-Kaspa, Y.
1989   Jet-Probes. Pp. 235–38 in Raban 1989.

The Joint Expedition to Caesarea Maritima Eleventh Season, 1984

ROBERT J. BULL
Drew University
Madison, NJ 07940

EDGAR M. KRENTZ
Luthern School of Theology at Chicago
Chicago, IL 60615

OLIN J. STORVICK
Concordia College
Moorhead, MN 56560

MARIE SPIRO
University of Maryland
College Park, MD 20742

Archaeological evidence that the earliest streets of Caesarea Maritima were laid out orthogonally and that the city was built with its earliest structures set in rectiliniar blocks or insulae, *enabled the Joint Expedition to Caesarea to project a tentative street plan within the arc of the city's defense wall. By stratigraphic excavation, in widely separated* insulae *located across the site, the 1984 Expedition was able to clarify the street plan, further identify certain of the structures and installations found within the city plan and demonstrate their relationship to already excavated or partially excavated remains. As a result, the city's industrial (Field B), public (Field C), residential (Field G), and religious (Field O) installations were more precisely defined and related to one another.*

THE HERODIAN ORTHOGONAL CITY PLAN AT CAESAREA

The discovery at Caesarea Maritima of a columned north-south street or *cardo*, designated Cardo I West,[1] that extended north from the exit or *vomitorium* of the Herodian theater and that had been intersected at intervals along its length by east-west cross-streets, *decumani*, was the first clear indication of Herodian orthogonal street design at Caesarea Maritima (fig. 1). Remnants of a second north-south street, Cardo II West, were discovered in front of, and contiguous to, a series of Herodian barrel vaulted warehouses or *horrea*, built along the Caesarea sea front. The line of vaults and the street remains determined the north-south course of Cardo II West and established that it had been laid out parallel to Cardo I West. Subsequent examination of the site determined that *decumani* formed the northern and southern limits of city blocks, *insulae*, and intersected the north-south streets, *cardinese*, at right

angles in all of the intersections uncovered in Areas C, N, K, M and L (fig. 1). The fact that both *decumani* in *cardinese* had been built contiguous to, or laid out in relation to, *insulae* or structures datable to the Herodian period, lends credence to Josephus' assertion that Herod had laid out the city of Caesarea according to a "magnificent plan" (Josephus, *Ant.* XV:331).

Using as evidence both the location and relation of partially excavated streets and intersections, a grid plan of the city's streets was projected across the entire site. Central to that grid plan was the projection of a north-south street along a line, the width of an *insula* to the east of Cardo I West, that located a street, *cardo*, proximate to the eastern edge of the Crusader Fortress and, in its northern extension, between the two round towers that formed the northern gate of the Herodian city wall. The course of this *cardo*, on plan, was central to the Herodian city, was related to *insulae* dated to the Herodian period, was the longest of the *cardinese* within the projected city wall, and exited

63

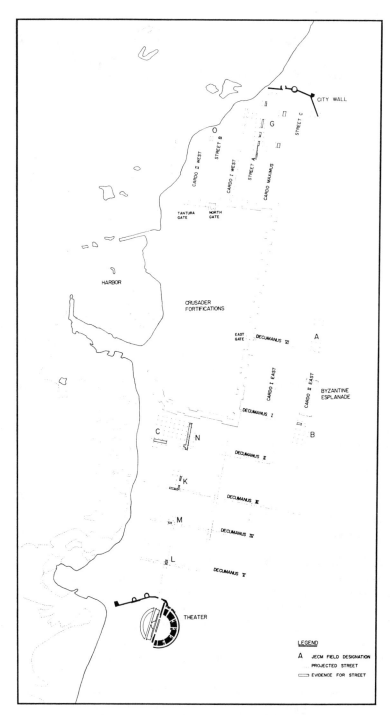

Fig. 1. Projected city street plan of Caesarea Maritima.

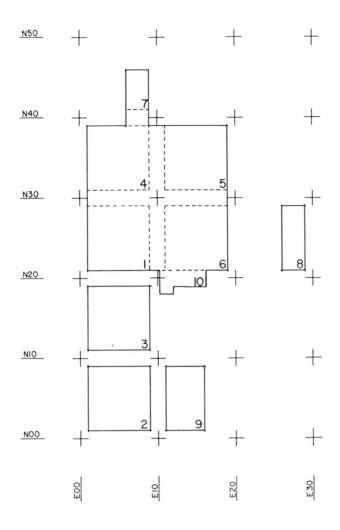

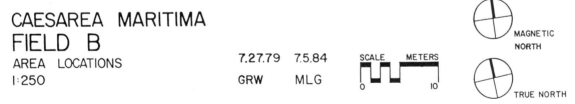

CAESAREA MARITIMA
FIELD B
AREA LOCATIONS
1:250

7.27.79   7.5.84

GRW   MLG

SCALE   METERS

MAGNETIC
NORTH

TRUE NORTH

Fig. 2. Location Plan of excavated Areas in Field B.

the city at a point in the northern wall where a major gate was found. For these reasons the projected *cardo* was designated the Cardo Maximus of Herodian Caesarea.

Based upon the newly derived, if still tentative, orthogonal city plan and the stratigraphic examination undertaken during the past ten seasons of

excavation and research at Caesarea, the Joint Expedition to Caesarea has developed the clearest archaeological history of Herodian Caesarea to date. This enhanced archaeological history and the clearer understanding of the plan and profile of the early city that it afforded, served as the basis for the planning and undertaking of the 1984 excavation.

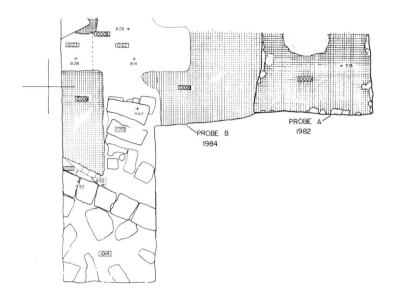

CAESAREA MARITIMA
B.10 PROBES
FINAL TOP PLAN
MLG 7.27.82, 6.21.84   MR 6.19.89
© 1984, THE JOINT EXPEDITION TO CAESAREA MARITIMA

1:20

SCALE   METERS
0   1   2

Fig. 3. Location Plan of Probe A and Probe B in Areas 6 and 10 of Field B.

FIELD B

In all previous seasons of excavations in Field B (1971, 1972, 1974, 1978, and 1982), evidence of industrial activity from the Early Islamic period was found (Bull *et al.* 1987: 11–31; Toombs 1987: 17–21). Included in that evidence were the remains of two furnaces (Area 6) and a kiln (Area 8), each surrounded by large quantities of slag, waster, and pottery fragments, both glazed and unglazed.

In 1982, to gain additional evidence of pottery and glazing in Field B, Probe A, was cut into the balk between Area 6 and Area 10 (figs. 2, 3) and the stratigraphy of the kiln residue and the debris tip lines examined. The angle of repose of the debris indicated that the elevation and direction from which it had been thrown was south of Area 6 and from a height in Area 10. Household ceramics, glazed ware and slag found in the balk were the same kinds that had been found earlier in the industrial debris of Area 6 and other contiguous Areas in Field B (Bull *et al.* 1991: 5f.).

In 1984, Probe B, located to the west of Probe A (fig. 3) sought to further delineate the industrial debris found in the balk between Areas 6 and 10 and its relationship to the 1.50 m wide stone wall, Wall 10114, that ran diagonally across the northern sector of Area 10. Seven superimposed layers of debris, gravity-laid rubble, lime, and plaster-filled earth were excavated down to Surface 10009, the same patterned mosaic surface previously uncovered in Areas 3, 4, and 6 and one that has been identified as part of a late sixth or early seventh century C.E. street. The layers of tumbled wall stones, reddish clay, charcoal, slag, and lime, contained a very high concentration of fragments from cook pots, skillets, casseroles, and lamps. Both skillets and casseroles had a light to dark, honey-colored glaze on their cooking surfaces; and many sherds from those and similar vessels bore evidence of burning. Large numbers of lamps, wasters, and lamp fragments were recovered. Of the lamp fragments, sherds from spur-handled Islamic lamps were most frequent. Three pentagonal, spur-

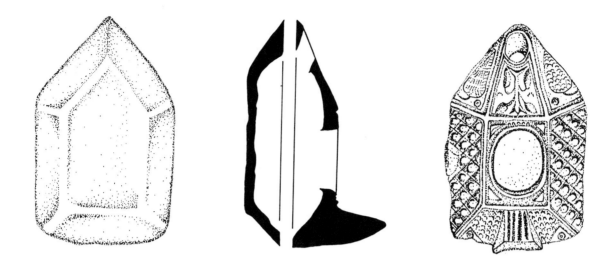

NINTH-CENTURY SPUR-HANDLED LAMP

C '74   C '84   C '84   C '84
B.6.47   B.10.166   B.10.161   B.10.0
5.23.9   17   1   7.24.1

AR
© 1984, THE JOINT EXPEDITION TO CAESAREA MARITIMA

Fig. 4. Drawing of ninth-century spur-handled lamp.

handled, ninth century Islamic lamps, of a type otherwise rare but relatively common at Caesarea, were uncovered, all from the same mold (fig. 4).

The high index of household pottery made of the same red clay, the concentration of wasters, the remains of kiln furniture, and the wide and deep layers of kiln debris, point to the presence of an industrial area that included the manufacture of pottery in the eighth to ninth century C.E. in Field B at Caesarea.

FIELD C

Field C is the *insula* that lies immediately south of the Crusader fortress and includes the northernmost of the four high stationary sand dunes that line the shore between the Crusader Fortress and the Roman theater (fig. 1). Excavation in Field C since 1972 has recovered sections of Cardo I West and Cardo II West; Decumanus II which intersects both *cardenes*; a series of *horrea* (warehouses) that open on Cardo II West; as well as, the remains of public and semi-public Roman and Byzantine structures built on top of Vaults 1 through 12 (fig. 5). The 1984 season sought to answer questions raised by those findings and to fill gaps in our knowledge of the *insula* by using different approaches to four problem areas.

ROMAN BARREL VAULTS BUILT AS HORREA

In 1973 Vault 1 was discovered in Field C, Areas 7, 8, and 11 beneath Roman building remains and dune sand. The first of a series of large (5 m by 5 m by 30 m) Roman barrel vaults, Vault 1, was constructed in the first century B.C.E. as a *horreum* (warehouse) and reconstructed in the second century C.E., as a Mithraeum. Efforts begun in

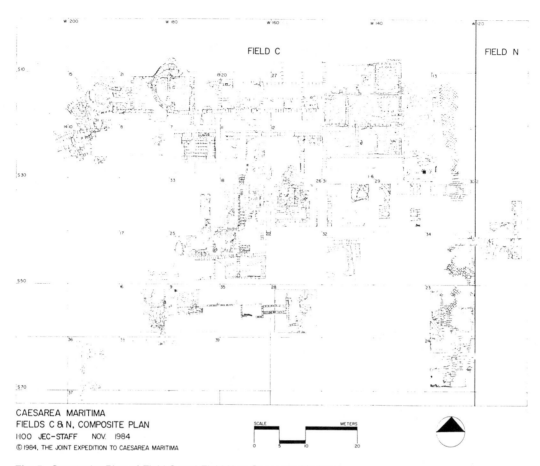

Fig. 5. Composite Plan of Field C and Field N at Caesarea Maritima.

1974 to examine the entire complex of *horrea* that front on Cardo II West and Decumanus II (fig. 6), resulted in 12 vaults being entered, examined, and recorded. Four vaults, Vaults 1, 2, 11, and 12, the largest vaults found, were built contiguous to one another and of the same dimensions and construction. The other eight vaults varied in size, construction or reconstruction, and in some instances, orientation. All twelve vaults had suffered damage or collapse to some degree; due, it was assumed, to earthquake action. Vaults 2, 11, and 12 were considered possible excavation targets from which The Joint Expedition could recover evidence, especially ceramic evidence, that would help determine whether or not the vault had been built as, or had been used as, *horrea*. Vault 2 was entered with difficulty and found to be the most completely collapsed of any of the vaults. In Vault 11 only a short section of its length had been preserved because a heavy relieving arch had been built interior to its eastern end. Vault 12 was entered in Field C, Area 25 through the top of its vaulting. It was dis-

covered that approximately one third of its eastern end remained intact because a massive relieving vault had been constructed there. The part of the ceiling in Vault 12 not supported by the relieving vault, but above the area where excavation could best occur, had become so weakened and depressed that the vault's ceiling appeared concave to those of us who first entered it (fig. 7). Though no excavation was attempted in Vault 12 in the 1984 season, due to the extreme danger of collapse, details gained from Vaults 1, 2, 11, and 12 confirm our belief that the four vaults were originally built as *horrea*.

Phase 7, Roman (10 B.C.E.–330 C.E.)

Vault 12 antedates the building of Structure 2, the Honorific Building related to the Mithraeum in Vault 1, and supports the southern arm of that U-shaped structure. The western end of Structure 2 has broken off at the point where the vaulting beneath it collapsed (fig. 8). It is probable, based on

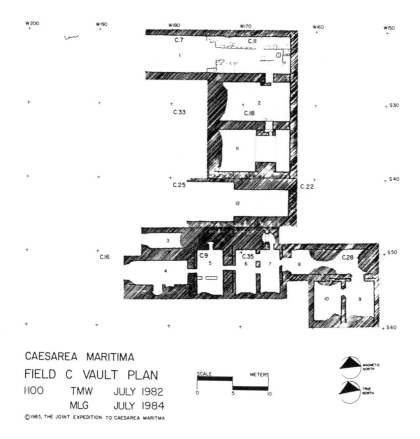

CAESAREA MARITIMA

FIELD C VAULT PLAN

1:100   TMW   JULY 1982
             MLG   JULY 1984
©1983, THE JOINT EXPEDITION TO CAESAREA MARITMA

SCALE   METERS
0   5   10

MAGNETIC NORTH

TRUE NORTH

Fig. 6. Plan of twelve vaults located in Field C.

the size, location, and construction that the four large vaults, Vaults 1, 2, 11, and 12, all of which support Structure 2, constitute a series of four *horrea* dating from the first century B.C.E.

Phase 6, Byzantine (330–640 C.E.)

Vaults 3 through 10 vary greatly in size, construction, and arrangement, when compared to Vaults 1, 2, 11, and 12. They form an interrelated complex of vaults with evidence of extensive rebuilding and adaptation. They contain well preserved frescoe remains, including several with Christian symbols (crosses in various styles and a large cartoon of a fresco of 12 figures with nimbuses in Vault 9). In order to help date the complex, a probe was dug in the bottom of Vault 9. It revealed a flagstone floor laid on earth, which in turn overlay three earlier surfaces of packed soft limestone. Pottery from beneath the pavement and from within the packed surfaces dated to the Byzantine period.

These and other findings suggest that Vaults 3 through 10 were constructed or reconstructed on the remains of destroyed vaults that originally stood in the south-eastern corner of the *insula*, that

is, Field C. The destroyed vaults, some similar in construction to Vaults 1, 2, 11, and 12, were probably destroyed by earthquake action; the same action that damaged all of the twelve vaults found in Field C. The complex of small vaults, Vaults 3 through 10, used the earlier vault material in their reconstruction and adaptation. Vaults 5, 6, and 7, perhaps part of the original vault plan, served to buttress the lateral thrust of the larger vaults to the north. Vaults 8, 9, 10, and an as yet unexamined vault west of Vault 10, were additions to the vault complex that fronted on Cardo II West. Of the rebuilt vaults, two or perhaps three, had doorways that opened on Decumanus II. The reconstructed vaults found limited use as warehouses but extensive other use by the Christian community. After the Islamic occupation of Caesarea, the Christian frescos, especially those in Vault 9, were covered with thick coats of plaster, thus preserving them.

BYZANTINE STREET PLAN

Much effort was expended in clarifying the streets that bounded the *insula* in Field C. The

Fig. 7. Internal view of Vault 12, looking east. The relieving vault, shown here, was constructed internal to Vault 12 in order to prevent its collapse.

Byzantine *cardo* first discovered in 1974 was carefully cleared with a backhoe for a stretch of 40 m from Area 13 in the north to the east-west *decumanus*, Decumanus II, on the south side of the *insula*. While the street surface is not completely preserved, enough survives to measure accurately the width of the carriageway. As fig. 5 shows, the paving is not consistent. The paving stones are laid in a herringbone pattern in Areas 13 and 40, change to an ashlar style in Area 30, return to a herringbone pattern in Areas 34 and 23, and change back again to the ashlar pattern as they intersect with Decumanus II in Area 24. The pavers of Cardo I West were laid in a herringbone pattern, except where the *cardo* ran up or down a slope. In Area 30, where the *cardo* is slightly inclined, the pavers are laid in parallel rows across the width of the street. It is assumed that the parallel, transverse lines, formed by the interstices between the pavers, afforded better traction on a slope than did the herringbone pattern, especially in wet weather. Other construction features found in the street in Areas 30, 23, and 24 are not clear. Additional excavation in Areas 29, 34, and others will be needed to further define Cardo I West and the intersection with Decumanus II.

We also investigated Cardo II West in Area 10, which ran along the waterfront and in front of the line of vaults in Field C and we were able to clarify the intersection of Cardo II West with Decumanus II in Areas 36 and 37. In addition, we probed for Cardo II West in front of the presumed entrance to Vault 1 in Area 10. The street pavers immediately in front of the entrance had been used as the foundation for structures related to the bath (Area 10 and 15), which date from the Late Byzantine period. Since we were not able to penetrate below the street surface, we cannot yet date the laying of the pavement. While all of Cardo II West was not uncovered, we can now measure the east-west dimension of the Field C *insula* and with the discovery of Decumanus II, we can plot the southern boundary of that *insula*.

THE BYZANTINE PROVINCIAL TAX OFFICE AND RELATED STRUCTURES

Two projects were related to the clarification of these structures. M. Spiro of the University of Maryland spent much time studying, photographing, and recording the mosaic pavements; and S. Bonde of Brown University studied the surviving architecture of Structure 1 (fig. 20) in order to phase the building in its various stages of use. A separate report will be made on those studies.

To clarify the history of Field C, we excavated Area C 20, the only remaining unexcavated area on the north side of the Field C *inaula*, and removed all balks between Areas 15 through 13 (fig. 9).

Phase 7a, Late Roman (200–330 c.e.) or Phase 6c, Early Byzantine (330–450 c.e.)

Street 20056, composed of packed chalk about 0.10 m thick, survives for a length of about 25 m

Fig. 8. Western end of the intact remains of Vault 12 found in Field C, Area 25.

and averages about 2.50 m in width. It was broken by Wall 20054 in the west (fig. 10) and by the apsidal structure (Areas 19 and 21) that destroyed its westward extension to Cardo II West; in the east, Structure 1 was erected over it. It was lined by rooms or shops formed by regularly spaced Walls 27091 and 27092 running north-south on either side. The rooms averaged about 3.30 m wide and 3.40 m deep, typical for shops in that period. Only the very lowest courses of those walls remain and the flooring of one room survives in only one small patch of *opus sectile* pavement. The dating of the street is difficult, but the best evidence at present is two mid-fourth century coins found in the makeup for the pavement. On the other hand, the foundation trench of Wall 20095 contained only Roman sherds (some possibly Byzantine on ware).

Phase 6a, Late Byzantine (550–640 C.E.)

The north side of the Field C *insula* underwent a major change in the Middle or Late Byzantine period. The apsidal structure (fig. 9) was begun at its western end and Structure 1 was built over Street 20056 to the east.

Interpretation of the later phases in Area 20 has been made difficult due to the building of a modern access road along the northern edge of Field C. Construction equipment, in the course of building the street, destroyed much of Wall 20010, everything north of it, and a large amount of everything south of it except for fragments of walls built against Wall 20010. East-west Wall 20084, laid on top of Wall 20088, north-south Wall 20086, on Wall 20090, and Wall 20085 on Wall 20089 are evidence for a room (fig. 10). It is unclear whether these walls are two phases of a structure or a single phase of stepped construction. The room apparently extended into Street 20056, whose Surface 20070 was crudely repaired. It is clear that at one time the area was used by the potter whose workshop was discovered earlier in Areas 19 and 21, since Floor 20064 was covered with hard-packed chalk, filled with Late Byzantine amphorae (fig. 11) of the same type as found in Areas 19 and 21. A second phase in the same room is represented by Pavers 20071 laid over the hard-packed layer with amphora fragments and may represent the use of the room after the Persian destruction of 614 C.E.

Areas 27 and 20 both contained a series of hydraulic installations: a pool and associated spillwater channel in Area 27 (and a small pond); and a water channel that came into the area from the south, dropped to the level of Pavement 20056 through a spillway and ran north through Channel 20073 in Area 20. No traces, however, remain of the circulation pattern between the public structure and these related water installations and pavement.

Phase 4, Byzantine-Islamic (ca. 640 C.E.)

The heavy destruction layer that reflects the Islamic conquest of 640 C.E. is represented by two distinct layers of destruction debris that covered Walls 20084, 20085, 20086, 20089, 20088, and 20090. Layer 20024 was filled with roof tile and marble architectural fragments, and Layer 20025 contained more ash and potsherds. The latest sherds in those *loci* are Late Byzantine, and the latest coin dates from 616–627 C.E.

Phases 3–1, Pre-Crusader Islamic to Modern (640 C.E.–Present)

Again, interpretation is difficult because of the disturbance caused by the modern road, but there was a clear buildup of earth over the area after the Islamic conquest, while the area between Wall

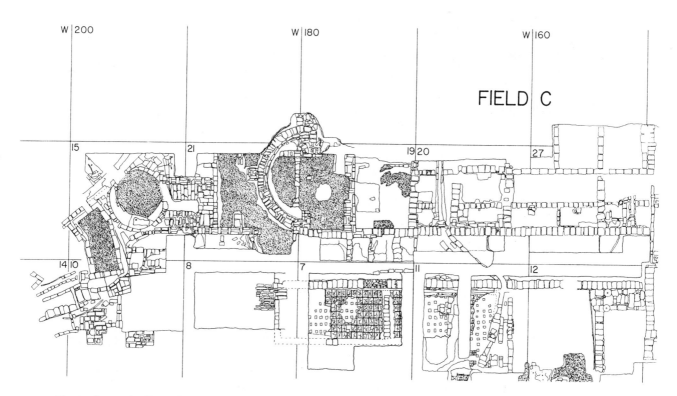

Fig. 9. Composite Plan of Areas excavated in northern third of Field C.

20010 and the south balk showed the use of Field C as a cemetery into the Ottoman period. North of east-west Wall 20010, all later remains were disturbed.

THE BYZANTINE CARDO

The excavation of Field C, Areas 5 and 6 in 1972, Area 13 in 1974, and Areas 23 and 24 in 1978 suggested that Cardo I West was a *via columniata* or *tecta* with a continuous pedestrian walkway on its western side. Evidence for a pedestrian walkway on the east was recovered in Field K. The 1976 discovery of Pier 5137 (later extended to the east by one course of stone), whose south and east faces were plastered, and the subsequent discovery of a crude addition, Wall 5135, laid on top of the well-cut stones of Wall 5156, suggested a very complicated architectural history for the southern third of Area 5 (fig. 12). We partially excavated Area 5 in 1982 and returned in 1984 to learn the relationship of structures in Area 5 to Structure 1 (the Municipal Archive Building), Cardo I West, and those structures found in Area 29. We do not yet know how the architecture in Area 5 is related to Structure 1, but we have concluded that Cardo I

West had neither a colonnade nor a pedestrian walkway at this point since a room here opened directed onto Cardo I West.

Phase 7, Late Roman (200–330 C.E.)

The remains of the Roman period are sparse and puzzling. Stones 5174 and 5179 (fig. 12) represent either the lowest course of a Roman wall or the foundation for street curbing earlier than the Byzantine Cardo. More puzzling still is Wall 5157, the northward extension of Wall 29005, which survived to two courses. In both Areas 5 and 29, the foundation trenches for Wall 29005 indicate that it was laid in soil that contained predominantly Roman sherds, with some Byzantine based on ware. Next to the wall was a crude surface resting on soil containing Byzantine and Middle Islamic pottery. It is difficult to account for Wall 5157 and its associated pottery unless one assumes that earth fill was brought in containing the Roman pottery.

Phase 6, Main Byzantine (330–640 C.E.)

Pier 5137 is the north wall of a room bounded by Wall 5139 on the west and Wall 5189 on the

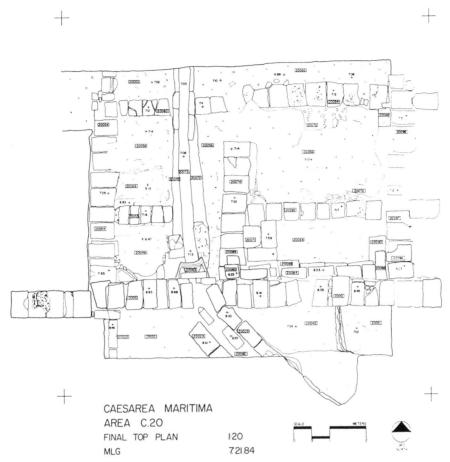

Fig. 10. Top Plan of Field C, Area 20.

south. The room had benches in front of Pier 5137 and in Locus 5188 in front of Wall 5189. Further, the room had a mosaic floor that appears to date from the fourth or fifth centuries C.E. on stylistic grounds. The relation of the floor to Cardo I West is suggested by a fragment of a mosaic inscription in *tabula ansata* to be read as one entered the room from the street. This makes it impossible for either a pedestrian walkway or colonnade to have fronted this room. It may well have served as a "guard-room" or performed another function in relation to Structure 1, although we need to dismantle Platform 5152, Pier 5137, and probe to the north in order to establish the precise relationship.

When the latest pavement in the eastern forecourt of Structure 1 was laid during the Late Byzantine

Fig. 11. Amphorae found on floor of potters workshop in Field C, Area 20.

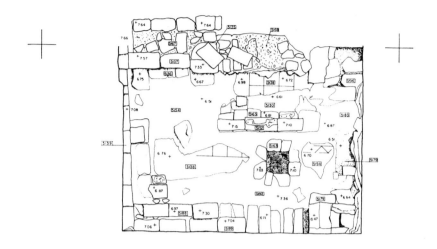

Fig. 12. Final Top Plan of Field
C, Area 5.

CAESAREA MARITIMA
AREA C.5
FINAL TOP PLAN   1:20
MR   8.8.84

period, heavy rubble concrete (*opus incertum*), Platform 5135, was built over mosaic Surface 5138,
partly destroying it.

Phase 3, Pre-Crusader Islamic (640–1200 C.E.)

Mosaic 5138 was further destroyed by Islamic
period Well 5164/82 dug through it in Early to
Middle Islamic times. Roughly 0.60 m square, the
well survives to a depth of 3.75 m. Finds from it
include a bronze porringer (6.18.03), five zoomorphic spouts, and a miniature Islamic lamp
(6.18.10) (fig. 13).

FIELD G

The Joint Expedition to Caesarea Maritima conducted excavations in three areas of Field G: Area
12, directly east of Area 7; Area 17, east of Area
13 and south of Area 9; and Area 18, directly south

of Area 7 (fig. 14). While each excavation had
specific goals, the general aim this season was the
elucidation of Street A (fig. 1) and adjacent structures. There now remain only two areas unexcavated in a 90 m line of squares stretching from
Area 5 in the north through Area 10 in the south on
the high ground lying between the Crusader fortress and the northern wall of the Herodian city.

Phase 7a, Late Roman (200–330 C.E.)

In Area 17, missing pavers where Street 17014
intersects the north balk permitted a small probe
into the material below street level (fig. 15). Late
Byzantine pottery was found above and below Surface 17028, supporting the dating already offered
for the street. At about 0.67 m below the street
level, a striated gray plaster surface was found
with Late Roman pottery below indicating that this
may have been part of a plaster street of the period
(fig. 16). The small area, however, precluded fur-

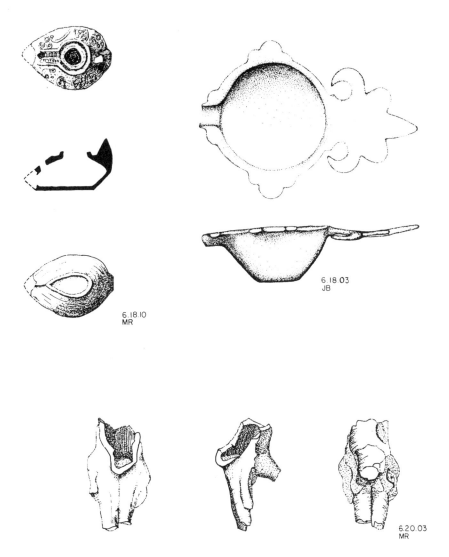

Fig. 13. Some of the small finds recovered from Well 5164/82 in Field C, Area 5 were a bronze porringer, several Islamic lamps, and zoomorphic clay spouts.

ther testing of that hypothesis until an additional part of the street is removed.

In Area 12, the major structure of the period is Street 12015 constructed of hard *mezzi* limestone pavers laid in a herringbone pattern with a depth of 0.20 m where the stones joined each other (fig. 17). Each stone also has a pointed bottom extending another 0.20 m which was laid into the sand and *hamra* mixture below. Along the eastern edge of the street was a small plaster surface. Pavers were removed on the north and south limits of the street and pottery was found dating to Late Roman period. This supports the conclusion that Street A was laid toward the middle of the fourth century c.e. Efforts to find a lower street proved fruitless

when bedrock was encountered about 0.55 m below the street elevation.

In the eastern part of the square, two Late Roman period walls were found. Wall 12057 runs north-south and consists of headers in the top course and dry-laid smaller stones in its lower courses. On the north it was cut by later Wall 12037 which used Wall 12057 as a foundation; and on the south, Wall 12057 abuts Wall 12062. The sand beneath the walls produced pottery generally no later than Late Roman, with a few sherds that might be called Byzantine. Hence, we concluded that the walls formed parts of one or more structures in the same phase as Street 12015, but the lack of material culture remains makes that suggestion only tentative.

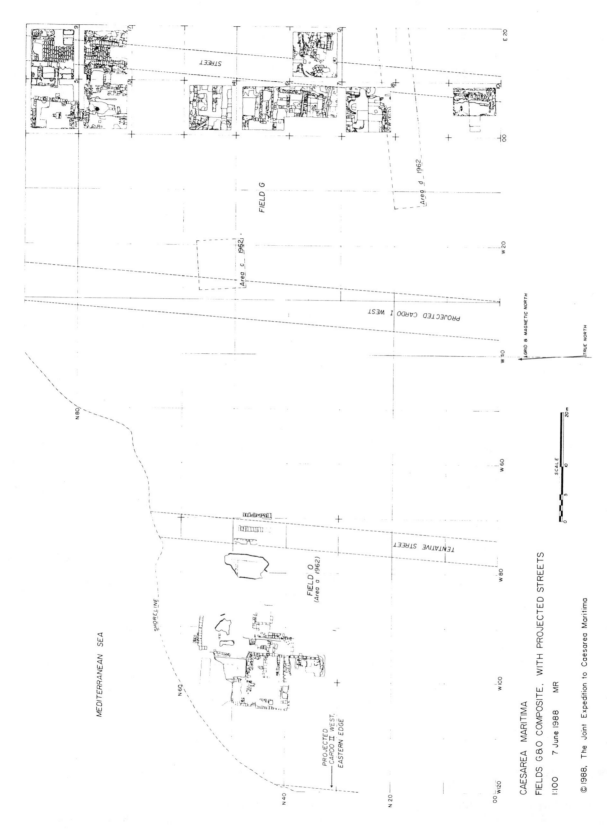

CAESAREA MARITIMA

FIELDS G&O COMPOSITE. WITH PROJECTED STREETS

1:100   7 June 1988   MR

© 1988, The Joint Expedition to Caesarea Maritima

Fig. 14. Composite Plan of excavated Areas in Field G and Field O and projected north-south streets.

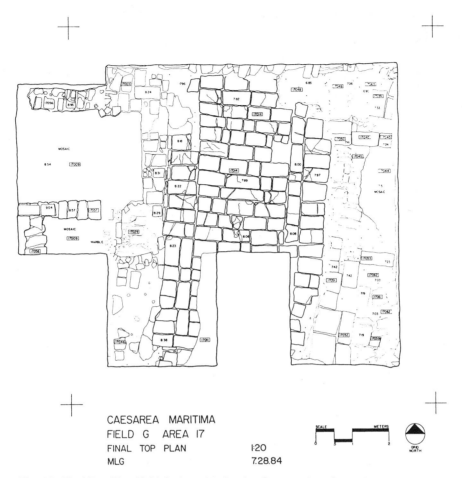

CAESAREA MARITIMA
FIELD G AREA I7
FINAL TOP PLAN 1:20
MLG 7.28.84

Fig. 15. Final Top Plan Field G, Area 17 showing Street 17014, Street A.

The major structure from this period in Area 18 is the east-west wall which was the target of the large robber trench that cut the square into northern and southern parts. The trench reached into the yellow sand and *kurkar* bedrock that elsewhere in Field G has been the founding level of Roman structures. Walls 18013, 18038, and 18009, and Surface 18037 were all cut by the large robber trench and only parts of the walls and a part of Surface 18037 remain, extending south from the north balk (fig. 18). Wall 18013 was reused in the Byzantine period, Wall 18038 has a north-south extent of 1.35 m, and Wall 18009 is represented by two flat stones with a north-south extent of 1.05 m. Surface 18037 serves as a makeup layer for later Surface 18012 and consists of gravelly soil with *hamra* chunks, bits of plaster, and random tesserae. It had an elliptical shape against Wall 18038 and the north balk, while on the east side of Wall 18038 it showed the same curve as Surface

18012 that accommodated the *tabun*. It is not clear what function that surface had in Late Roman times because of the later building of Surface 18012 on top of it.

In the southern half of the square, this phase is represented by a part of Wall 18009 (18049), by east-west Wall 18072, and by *Tabun* 18068. Wall 18049 consists of two stones in the top course with a total north-south dimension of 1 m. The pottery in the soil above the wall is Late Roman and the coin found lying on the wall was first century C.E. This wall aligns with Wall 18009 in the north and must be considered the southern part of the wall that was severed by the robber trench. It also aligns with Wall 7141 in the square to the north which was assigned a Middle Roman date. The discrepancy requires further analysis.

Wall 18072 is an east-west wall extending 4.80 m from the west balk but not quite parallel with Wall 18063, which later used part of it as a

Fig. 16. Photograph of Field G, Area 17 looking south. Street 17014, Street A, is to the right and the probe for an earlier street is to the left.

foundation. Pottery within Wall 18072 was Middle Roman, so it is safe to assign this wall at least to Late Roman.

Tabun 18068 is centered 4.25 m from the west balk, directly south of Wall 18072, and has a diameter of 1 m. The pottery in the tabun floor is Late Roman with a possible Roman/Byzantine call on ware, while that pottery directly below the overfloor is Middle Roman. Hence, the *tabun* is assigned to the Late Roman period (fig. 18).

There appear to be three ovens in Areas 7 and 18; each lies directly south of an east-west wall and is approximately the same distance from the east balk. The northern and southern ones can be definitely dated to the Roman period. The central one belongs to Late Byzantine, but there is the suggestion of an earlier *tabun* lying below it. The location of each *tabun* in each structure, the size and construction of the buildings, and the mosaics in Area 17, all seen as components of residences, have enabled us to view Field G as an area of domestic rather than public construction.

Phase 6c, Early Byzantine (330–450 C.E.)

Excavation of the 2 m area lying east of Street 17014 in Area 17 revealed a pervasive and heavy plaster fall that contained Late Byzantine pottery. Removal of the debris disclosed mosaic Surface 17044, about 0.85 m beneath street level. The mosaic extends 2.80 m north-south, where it is bounded on the north by Wall 17043 in the north and Wall 17053 in the south. The area to the west of the mosaic is filled with two rows of large stones, Locus 17051, one of headers and the other of stretchers. To examine those stones would require removal of either street or mosaic, or both, so no dating can presently be offered except to suggest that they belong to the same phase as the mosaic structure and should, therefore, be assigned either to Early Byzantine or Late Roman periods (fig. 15).

In Area 12, Wall 12037 extends 4.80 m from the east balk where it was cut by a robber trench. Since the locus below was predominantly Roman with a few sherds of Byzantine ware, and the wall lies over Late Roman Wall 12078, it seems best to assign this wall to the Early Byzantine phase, although no other structures in Area 12 were found associated with it (fig. 17).

Phase 6b, Middle Byzantine (450–550 C.E.)

The only element in Field G that can be assigned to this phase is tessellated Surface 17009 (also found in Area 13 in 1982) and its associated northern Wall 17056 in Area 17. With the removal of the balk between Areas 13 and 17, the preserved extent is 3.80 m north-south and 3.30 m east-west. The mosaic clearly runs against east-west Wall 17056 on the north, which is comprised of irregularly squared stones in two rows laid on a foundation course. Later the surface was cut in the southwest corner by Walls 17057 and 17058. No probe has been made beneath the mosaic so no stratigraphic evidence can be offered for its dating, but the pottery in the fill around Walls 17057/58 is Late Byzantine (fig. 15).

Phase 6a, Late Byzantine (550–640 C.E.)

Considerable activity must be assigned to this phase, given the number of structures from all three squares. In Area 17, three plaster and cobble Surfaces 17007, 17021, and 17011 (which adjoined stone Structure 17010) all appear to be part

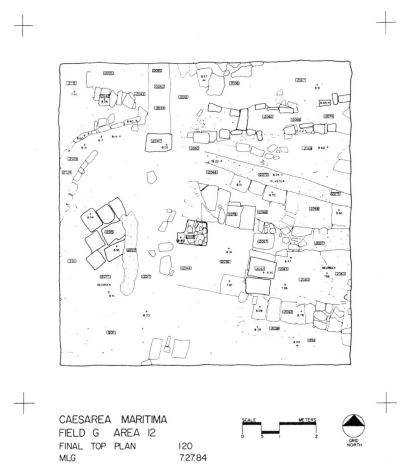

CAESAREA MARITIMA
FIELD G   AREA 12
FINAL TOP PLAN   1:20
MLG   7.27.84

Fig. 17. Final Top Plan Field G, Area 12 showing location of Street 12015's limestone pavers laid in herringbone pattern.

of a complex that represents a dwelling and courtyard lying above the street at some time when the street was no longer in use, at least to its present width.

The major structure of this period in Area 17 was the continuation southward of the street found in Area 9. The street slopes to the north, accommodating the general terrain, and the limestone curbstones and pavers are of similar size, generally laid as stretchers perpendicular to the axis of the road. The roadway is 2.50 m wide and the road with curbers is 4.50 m wide. A feature unique to Area 17 is the additional row of curbers inside the curbstones on the east side of the street. No pavers were lifted, but missing paving stones permitted excavation below street level. Since Late Byzantine pottery was found in the third locus down, assignment of the street to this phase seems warranted. Note that the same dating was made for the street in Area 9 during the 1982 excavations. Small

areas of plaster surface were found just above the street level and probably represent living surfaces after the street went out of use (fig. 15).

In Area 12, Drain 12058 was found running east-west from the east balk before it was cut by the previously mentioned robber trench. Four cappers were in place but most of the drain was exposed. Probes beneath the drain bottom failed to provide secure dating within the Late Byzantine period, although the pottery showed general Byzantine characteristics. Since the elevation on the east is about the same as the street, this drain cannot have been in use when the street was in use; or at least the drain did not run under the street. Another drain, Drain 12028, in the western portion of the square, seems to align with Drain 12058 but is about 0.50 m lower and so could not have been an extension of drain 12058. Drain 12028 could have run under the street, but the drain could not be dated securely (fig. 17).

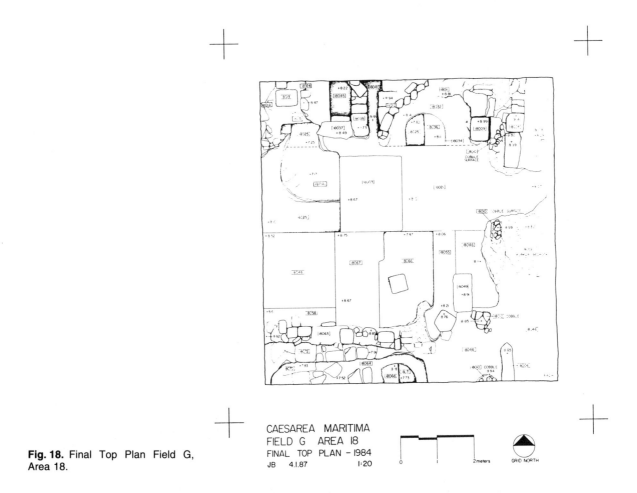

CAESAREA MARITIMA
FIELD G   AREA 18
FINAL TOP PLAN – 1984
JB   4.1.87   1:20

0   1   2 meters   GRID NORTH

Fig. 18. Final Top Plan Field G, Area 18.

In Area 18, the Late Byzantine structures are numerous and at one time covered the entire square, but subsequent robber activity has cut them into northern and southern parts. Along the north balk are two walls, cobble surfaces, and a *tabun*. Wall 18006 runs north-south about 2.25 m and is constructed of various sized stones in a gray mortar. Adjacent to the west is a fragment of plaster and cobble Surface 18010 that appears to be associated with this wall. Another plaster and cobble surface, Surface 18012, was constructed with a curving arc surrounding *Tabun* 18034. In the northeast side of the oven, a semicircular hole penetrated its base, and a broken vessel was placed to function as a flue. Pottery from beneath the oven dates it to this phase; and pottery from the same period, along with third and fourth century coins was found in the fill behind the oven.

One difficulty is that cobbled Surface 18012 is about 0.90 m above the floor of the oven. Surface 18012 is bounded on the west by Wall 18013 and between Wall 18013 and the west balk lies plaster

and cobble Surface 18014. These last two structures have not been dated by pottery but their assignment to Phase 6a is suggested by their position and character. South of the robber trench, two small sections of Wall 18006 and cobble Surface 18010 were also found. In addition, the locus below Wall 18063, which parallels the south balk, contained primarily Late Byzantine pottery while the next locus below had only Roman pottery. Furthermore, the three soil loci directly above plaster and cobble Surface 18056, lying north of Wall 18063, as well as pottery within and below the surface, date primarily to Late Byzantine with a few sherds from the Byzantine-Islamic horizon. In addition, 45 coins found on the surface date from the third to fifth centuries C.E. This surface is slightly higher than the other surfaces and, perhaps, should be assigned to the Byzantine-Islamic phase. However, it seems to form a coherent whole with other Late Byzantine structures in the square and so further examination of the pottery is suggested (fig. 18).

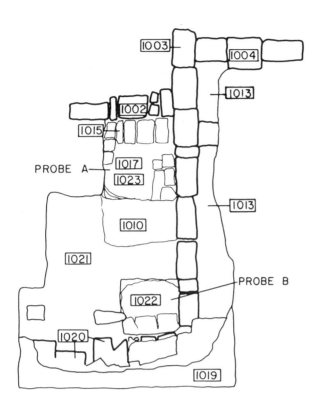

CAESAREA MARITIMA
FIELD O,   AREA 1
TOP PLAN   MLG
7.29.84

METERS
0 .5 1   2

GRID
NORTH

Fig. 19. Field O, Area 1, Final Top Plan.

Phase 5, Latest Byzantine (614–640 C.E.)

No activity can be assigned confidently to this phase.

Phase 4, Byzantine-Islamic (ca. 640 C.E.)

The only candidate for inclusion in this period was discussed in Phase 6a, Late Byzantine.

Phases 3b–3c, Pre-Crusader Islamic (640–900 C.E.)

All three areas showed Islamic materials in the upper two soil loci. Their activity in Phase 3b–3c is documented in Area 12 by a presumed robber trench that ran north-south along the east side of Street 12015, effectively cutting the square into

east and west parts. In Area 18, the robber activity was more extensive. Robbery of a large east-west wall running about 2 m south of the north balk cut the square into two parts and also cut some of the structures that survive along the north balk. Similar robberies of Walls 18006, 18009 (18049), and 18013 were also discovered. In the western side of Area 18 a coin was found that dated to 750 C.E. A note on the general disturbance during the Islamic period is the fact that some sherds found in Area 18 made joins of ancient breaks with sherds found in Areas 12 and 17; the latter being 50 meters distant.

Phases 1–3a, Post-Crusader-Fatimid and Seljuk (900–1300 C.E.)

No material culture remains were found that could substantiate occupation during these phases.

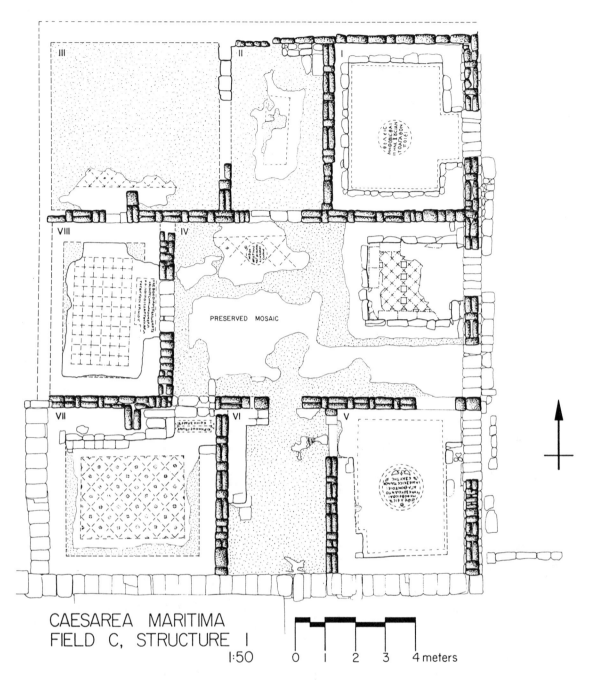

Fig. 20. Plan of Mosaics in Field C, Structure I, The Archives Building.

FIELD O

In 1984 the Joint Expedition received permission to undertake a limited excavation project in an area located approximately 70 meters west of Field G where in-depth excavations were conducted by M. Avi-Yonah of The Hebrew University in 1956 and 1962. The well constructed multiple room wall remains in the area, as well as such associated artifacts as menorah-adorned Corinthian capitals, superimposed mosaic floors, and lithic and mosaic inscriptions, led Avi-Yonah and others before him to conclude that the remains represented more than one synagogue, the latest synagogue dated, perhaps to the sixth century C.E. (Avi-Yonah 1956; 1960; 1963). Unfortunately, the available written and photographic evidence of this earlier work is meager and often unclear or contradictory.

Work by the Joint Expedition in 1982 in this area, designated Field O, was limited to a clearing operation and the production of a "stone-for-stone" drawing of those structures excavated earlier by Avi-Yonah. A plan of the structures in Field O when placed on the grid plan of the city showed not only the relationship of the structures in Field O to others excavated in Field G but also to a projected north-south street, tentatively identified as Street B, that was parallel to other north-south streets of the city. The orientation of the partially preserved mosaic at the eastern side of Field O and the remains of a north-south sewer helped establish the orientation and location of the projected street (fig. 14). The Joint Expedition 1984 license permitted excavation only outside the area of Avi-Yonah's previous work. Accordingly, Area 1 (fig. 19) sought to provide further stratigraphic evidence for the defining of structures in Field O through a small-scale excavation just to the south of the walls partly cleared by Avi-Yonah, Loci 1002, 1003, 1004.

Upon removal of the rubble from previous dumping, plaster Surface 1005 emerged in Probe A. Its subsequent removal revealed several more superimposed surfaces below: a polychrome marble surface of reused decorative architectural fragments cemented in *opus sectile* design in a heavy sand and hamra base and, beneath that surface, two more plaster surfaces, each with its associated makeup layer approximately 0.20 m in depth. The northern extent of those surfaces was contiguous to roughly laid east-west Wall 1015 lying just south of Wall 1002, excavated earlier. The associated pottery in these layers was predominantly Middle Byzantine.

Beneath the occupational surfaces in Probe A was a series of yellow sand layers lying on bedrock. The pottery in these loci was consistently Middle to Late Roman.

Expanded excavation to the south in Probe B revealed only that east-west Wall 1020 was constructed perpendicular to Wall 1003 and founded in yellowish sandy soil containing Middle and Late Roman pottery.

Conclusions from this season's work in Field O are tentative, given its limited extent. No evidence was found that could contribute to the problematic interpretation of the "synagogue" remains previously excavated. Nonetheless, it is possible to state several findings with some confidence. First, the consistent evidence of Middle Roman readings in those layers just above bedrock and adjacent to the foundation of Walls 1002, 1003, and 1004 would seem to place their construction in that period or

later. Second, there is evidence to the south and west of Walls 1002 and 1003 of Middle to Late Byzantine reconstruction that included a series of well constructed surfaces, some making use of earlier marble architectural fragments. This would be consistent with the number of mosaic or fragmentary marble surfaces uncovered at similar elevations and dated also by Avi-Yonah's work to the Late Byzantine period.

MOSAICS

Twenty-six mosaics were examined and recorded during the 1984 season. Of these 17 belong to the previously excavated Structure 1 in Field C (figs. 5 and 20). The building was completely cleared of overgrowth and all the walls and mosaics were cleaned so that the surfaces could be photographed in their architectural contexts. A survey of Rooms I–VIII followed in order to note the character and condition of the mosaics for a study of the architectural phases of the structure. Since a complete survey of the building could not be undertaken, the publication will have to be limited to a study of the latest architectural and decorative phases.

The mosaic surfaces in Structure 1 clearly reveal that the building underwent various reconstructions and redecoration. Each of the cleared floors revealed traces of earlier mosaics in Rooms I, II, V, and VI, and of a third level in Room VIII and in the probe in Room IV. Added to earlier evidence of two or more mosaic levels in Rooms IV and VIII, the finds provide the architectural evidence of multiple phases throughout Structure 1, except for Room VII, which revealed only one level. The single level there seems best explained by the assumption that an earlier floor, or floors, were removed when the hypocaust system was installed just to the west. That would also suggest that the building may have had a different function in its earlier phases. Indeed, the benches and shelves in Rooms I, II, V, VII, and VIII are later and were installed on or above earlier tessellated floors. Those rooms, therefore, lacked utilitarian furniture appropriate to a tax office, at least in their penultimate phase.

The earliest mosaic phase in Structure 1 appears in Rooms III and IV. Both pavements contain small, well-cut tesserae (1.2 cm^2) with a density averaging 56 to 58 tesserae per 10 cm square (56–58 per dm^2) in black geometric designs on a beige ground. The plain mosaic in Room I with its similar density and well-cut tesserae may belong to the

Fig. 21. Mosaic found in the dirt road west of Field G at the eroded shoreline of the Mediterranean.

same phase. Although the pavement in Room IV was covered by two later pavements, no trace of a later mosaic was found in Room III. The earlier mosaic may have continued in use or a later one may have been destroyed during construction of the modern public access road just to the north.

The latest paving phase is represented by the crude upper mosaic visible in Room IV with large tesserae (12 per dm²) as well as by the *opus sectile* pavement in the northeast sector of Room IV. The former extends as far as the pavers to the southeast and southwest and is datable stylistically to approximately the late sixth or early seventh century C.E. A probe in the area of the *sectile* floor in Room IV beneath the earlier tessellated paving and marble slabs yielded a coin of Julian (355–361 C.E.) and some Roman and Byzantine sherds. Thus, the marble paving phase of this room seems to belong to the sixth century C.E. Pending further evaluation of the architectural and stratigraphic evidence, the other mosaic phases in Structure 1 can be dated between the early part of the fifth century and the middle of the seventh century C.E.

At the request of A. Eitan, Director of the Department of Antiquities, the damaged mosaic with the Marinos inscription in Room IV was lifted in preparation for consolidation and cleaning. This work was supervised by Z. Barov, then Chief Conservator of Antiquities at the J. Paul Getty Museum. A probe through the mosaic foundations yielded sherds and one coin that will assist in the dating of the mosaic.

In Field C, Area 5 (fig. 12), three fragments of one pavement were uncovered, Mosaics 5154 and 5138. The two portions of Mosaic 5138 contain a straight grid with rather small tesserae (54 per dm²) while Mosaic 5154 bore a *tabula ansata* with two letters preserved of a two-line inscription. Both sections of Mosaic 5138 contain repairs: the northern one in red tesserae that replace the original black ones of the grid; the southern one in large white tesserae in the ground of the mosaic.

In Field G two mosaics were recorded in Areas 13 and 17 and one in the road west of Areas 15 and 16. In Area 17, Mosaic 17044 contained a design of tangent octagons composed of large red tesserae (25 per dm²). Although a plaster layer covering the mosaic is to be dated to the Late Byzantine period, the dating of the mosaic itself is problematic because it is utilitarian and the precise nature of its

Fig. 22. Southwest corner of The Bird Medallion Mosaic uncovered in Field Q, Area 1.

relationship to adjacent Street 17014 has not yet been determined. Its style is clearly not Middle or Late Byzantine. Whether it is to be identified as Late Roman or Early Byzantine awaits comparison with datable utilitarian pavements elsewhere at Caesarea. Its elevation lower than the street would certainly permit a Late Roman date.

Mosaic 17009 at the west side of Area 17 is decorative, not utilitarian. Its polychromy, designs, and tesserae (58 per dm^2) indicate a date no earlier than the middle to late fifth century C.E. Bordered by a two-strand guilloche in red, blue, and yellow, the interesting design of scattered red, pink, and ochre rosettes appears for the first time at Caesarea. That design and the section to the south with a pecking or fighting rooster appear to indicate the presence of a private or residential structure in the area. This hypothesis cannot be verified until more of the structure is cleared but evidence of other residences with decorative pavements have been uncovered in Field G. The mosaic found in the road to the west of Field G (fig. 21) may also belong to a private building. It is the most complex polychrome geometric design found to date. Framed by an ivy-leaf scroll border, the field con-

tains a dense design of "crosses of scuta" surrounded by rainbow bands, guilloches, and lozenges. It is executed with small, well-cut limestone and marble tesserae (70 to 78 per dm^2). A date in the middle of the fifth century C.E. or later can be assigned to this pavement.

Other mosaics were recorded in the Byzantine Esplanade and in Field B for comparative purposes. It has become quite clear that a very late school (550–650 C.E.) executed the mosaics in the areas cited above as well as in the upper level pavement at the eastern edge of Field O.

A final project of this session involved the very large "bird medallion mosaic" located several hundred meters east northeast of the Caesarea harbor on a low hill outside of the Byzantine defense wall. This large mosaic, thought by some to have been the floor of a "roofless church," was designated Field Q by the Joint Expedition. Probes dug through the sand overburden found the very colorful mosaic in a deteriorating condition. After this preliminary examination, we were concerned to examine, date, restore, and house the mosaic, if sufficient funds could be raised. J. Berman, Director of the California Museum of Ancient Art, and Z. Barov, Chief

Conservator of Antiquities at the J. Paul Getty Museum, visited the site to discuss a proposal for lifting and consolidating the mosaic. The project was supported by R. Bull, Director of the Joint Expedition, M. Spiro, Joint Expedition Mosaicist, and A. Eitan, Director of the Department of Antiquities. We uncovered a large portion of the mosaic (fig. 22) and confirmed the fact that lifting and consolidating the mosaic were necessary. It was our hope that this project could be undertaken in 1985, after the necessary archaeological and architectural surveys had been completed, a rather large sum of money raised, and a restoration team recruited. At the end of the session, the so called "bird medallion mosaic" in Field Q was again covered with sand.

NOTES

[1] When remains of streets were uncovered over several years of excavation by the Joint Expedition to Caesarea, the sections or parts of street discovered were identified by a locus number relevant to the Field and Area in which they were found. Since street remains and features associated with streets were discovered in more than half of the 111 Areas excavated, it became apparent that some street remains were part of a pattern that extended across the entire site. The Expedition's first efforts to define the grid plan of Caesarea and to name its streets were not very successful. Initially, north-south streets were labeled with Roman numerals, in the order of discovery and east-west streets were labeled with Arabic numerals, in the order of discovery. The Preliminary Report of the 1982 Joint Expedition to Caesarea published a projected city plan with the streets identified in this manner (Bull *et al.* 1982: fig. 1).

To avoid confusion and to identify the streets with the nomenclature used in the orthogonal plans of other first century cities, the streets of the Caesarea city plan used in this report and the ones adopted by the Joint Expedition are as follows: North-south streets are identified as *cardenes* and are numbered with Roman numerals, in order, east or west of a central Cardo, called the Cardo Maximus. East-west streets, identified as *decumani*, are numbered, in the order of discovery, with Roman numerals.

Several modifications of the orthogonal grid plan of Caesarea Maritima, developed by the Joint Expedition, have been used and published, frequently slightly altered and almost always without credit or citation.

[2] Institutions participating in the 1984 season were Brown University, Providence, RI; Concordia College, Moorhead, MN; Drew University, Madison, NJ; Emory & Henry College, Emory, VA; Loma Linda University, Riverside, CA; Luther Northwestern Theological Seminary, St. Paul, MN; Lutheran School of Theology at Chicago, Chicago, IL; University of Maryland, College Park, MD; Wake Forest University, Winston-Salem, NC; and Wilfrid Laurier University, Waterloo, Ontario; together with the sponsorship and participation of Earthwatch volunteers. This excavation was conducted under license from the Department of Antiquities of the State of Israel (A. Eitan, Director) and endorsed by the American Schools of Oriental Research.

Staff included: R. Bull, Director; E. Krentz, Associate Director; O. Storvick, Field Supervisor; V. Bull, Treasurer and Registrar; A. Palkovich, Anthropologist; M. Spiro, Mosaicist; S. Bonde, Architectural Historian; M. Govaars, Surveyor; P. Saivetz, Photographer; P. Lampinen, Numismatist.

Area supervisors in Field C were S. Bonde, M. Luker, and P. Lampinen; in Field G, M. Hilmer, J. Zink, J. Boyce, A. Shaffer, T. and H. Seawright and K. Gerhard; in Field B, V. Bailey; and in Field O, N. Goldman and H. Shirley.

BIBLIOGRAPHY

Avi-Yonah, M.
1963   Notes and News-Caesarea. *Israel Exploration Journal* 13: 146–48.
1960   The Synagogue of Caesarea: Preliminary Report. Pp. 44–48 in *Louis M. Rabinowitz Fund for the Exploration of Ancient Synagogues. Bulletin III.* Jerusalem: Hebrew University.
1956   Notes and News-Caesarea. *Israel Exploration Journal* 6: 260–61.

Blakely, J. A.
1989   The City Walls of Straton's Tower: A Stratigraphic Rejoinder. *Bulletin of the American Schools of Oriental Research* 273: 79–82.

Bull, R. J., Krentz, E. M., Strovick, O. J., Spiro, M.
1987   Chapter 15, 1978 Preliminary Report. In, *The Joint Expedition to Caesarea Preliminary Reports in Microfiche, 1971–1978.* Ed. R. J. Bull. Madison, NJ: Drew University.
1990   The Joint Expedition to Caesarea: Tenth Season, Preliminary Report. *Bulletin of the American Schools of Oriental Research. Research Supplement* 27: 69–94.

Josephus, Flavius
ca AD 94   The Antiquities of the Jews. *Loeb Classical Library,* 4–9, ed. H. St. J. Thackeray, R. Marcus, A. Wikgren, and L. Feldman. Cambridge, MA: Harvard University Press.

Toombs, L. E.
1987   Chapter 4, Field B, 1972, 1974 & 1976. Pp. 1–26 in, *The Joint Expedition to Caesarea Maritima: Preliminary Reports in Microfiche, 1971–1978.* Ed. R. J. Bull. Madison, NJ: Drew University.

Protohistoric Investigations at the Shiqmim Chalcolithic Village and Cemetery: Interim Report on the 1988 Season

THOMAS E. LEVY
Department of Anthropology
University of California, San Diego
La Jolla, CA 92093

DAVID ALON
Israel Antiquities Authority
Jerusalem, Israel

PAUL GOLDBERG
Peabody Museum, Harvard University
Cambridge, MA 02138

CAROLINE GRIGSON
The Royal College of Surgeons of England
London WC 2A 3PN, England

PATRICIA SMITH
Department of Anatomy,
Hadassah Medical Center
The Hebrew University of Jerusalem, Israel

JANE E. BUIKSTRA
Department of Anthropology
University of Chicago, U.S.A.

AUGUSTIN HOLL
Department of Ethnology and Prehistory
University of Paris X
Nanterre, France

YORKE ROWAN
Department of Anthropology
University of Texas at Austin

PAMELA SABARI
Department of Anatomy
Hadassah Medical Center
The Hebrew University of Jerusalem, Israel

The fall 1988 excavation at Shiqmim marked the second season of the Phase 2 investigations at this formative village and mortuary site. In the current report, new data are presented concerning the stratigraphic development of Shiqmim and its relation to the Beersheva Valley Chalcolithic culture. Quantitative data concerning the ceramic and lithic assemblages, archaeozoological samples, and the human remains are also analyzed.

INTRODUCTION

The Shiqmim Chalcolithic (ca. 4500–3500 B.C.E.) village and mortuary complex is located along the right bank of the Nahal (Wadi) Beersheva in the northern Negev desert of Israel. The site is one of the largest protohistoric sites in western Palestine and extends over an area of more than ten hectares. Since 1979, excavations have taken place at the site to examine the social and environmental processes that may have led to the emergence of social complexity in the northern Negev during the late fifth to early fourth millennia B.C.E. Beginning in 1987, the Phase 2 (1987–1989) investigations were initiated to explore the evolution of settlement in this portion of the Beersheva valley.

Taking a diachronic perspective, there were three goals of the 1988 season: excavation of the earliest occupation layers of the site to test for the presence of underground storage facilities and possible subterranean features similar to those found at Tell Abu Matar and Bir es-Safadi, sites located ca. 18 km upstream from Shiqmim along the Nahal Beersheva (cf. Perrot 1955; 1984); and stratigraphic excavation adjacent to the deep Eastern Trench (ca. 40 m long, 4 m wide, and maximum depth 6 m) dug by a bulldozer in 1987 (see Levy et al. 1990); and sampling of additional hill tops in the cemetery complex for mortuary structures and human remains to test hypotheses related to the social status, palaeopathology, and palaeonutrition of the Shiqmim community.[1]

THE VILLAGE EXCAVATIONS

Area C/Y

The 1988 excavations focused on the northern portion of the lower village, located on a terrace adjacent to the Nahal Beersheva. Eleven 5 × 5 m squares were opened in this area. In 1987, the deep trench profiles revealed numerous bell-shaped pits associated with possible crater-like depressions dug into the hard-packed Pleistocene loessial sediments that are confined to the northern portion of the site (Levy et al. 1990). By making several deep excavations in the area, we hoped to clarify the stratigraphic relationship between the subterranean and semisubterranean features observed in the deep section and the well-preserved rectilinear architecture that characterizes the upper stratum at the site. The main question focused on whether all those features were contemporaneous or whether there was evidence of clear stratigraphic change. The answer came from Square K/10 (figs. 1, 2), reopened after partial excavation in 1987. Two stratified well-built stone foundation walls dating from Stratum (Building Phase) I (Wall 226) and Stratum II (Wall 225) were found superimposed over a large crater-like feature with an unusually well-preserved wall (Wall 223) that could be clearly dated to Stratum III. Wall 223 had a stone foundation that reached a height of ca. 1.10 m and was capped by a wall of mudbrick ca. 1.0 m in height. This complete wall was thus ca. 2.10 m high and 0.60 m thick. A stone-lined niche on the east face of Wall 223 contained a small collection of beads. Dug into the floor of the crater-like feature were two bell-shaped pits (Loci 425 and 428)

filled with cultural debris (fig. 3). As these pits predate the Stratum II Wall 223, they are provisionally assigned to Stratum IV, the earliest settlement phase at Shiqmim. The stratigraphic picture obtained in Square K/10 reflects the general developmental picture found at Bir es-Safadi, where subterranean architectural features preceded the erection of the rectilinear buildings with stone foundations found close to the surface (Perrot 1984; Commenge-Pellerin 1990).

A cache of complete pottery vessels (Locus 412) was found facing Wall 223 in a pit sealed beneath a hard packed floor associated with Stratum III (figs. 2, 4). The cache contained ten vessels: one fenestrated stand; one high-neck bottle with flared rim; one jar with flared neck, multiple ear-handles, and richly painted geometric patterns; two small painted jars with short necks; one deep basin; and four V-shaped bowls. This season three pottery caches were found, bringing to four the total found at Shiqmim.

A number of human burials came to light in this area of the village. In Locus 431, an infant was found in a scatter of rubble. In Locus 437, an intentional secondary burial was exposed.

Area C/P

This area was opened on the northwestern limits of the village, at the top of the northern rise of the Pleistocene hillock. Six 5 × 5 m squares were opened. Only one square, G9/G10, showed clear evidence of semisubterranean and subterranean features. Here two walls (216 and 217), each measuring ca. 1.5 m in height, were used to line another semi-subterranean feature (Locus 515). These walls were made of small wadi cobbles, characteristic of the BP II construction style. At the base of this feature a large bell-shaped pit was found (Locus 577; fig. 5). These features seem to have been contemporary and were dug into the virgin Pleistocene sediments.

East of these features, a large depression was found; it had diameter of ca. 5 m, and was filled with light sandy soil and a complete Byzantine jar, cut into the Chalcolithic deposits. This represents the first large human-made disturbance dating from a historic period found at the site.

In the northern position of Area C/P, a packed clay "platform" (Locus 558) seems to date to Stratum II with reuse during Stratum I. A barrel-shaped pit (Locus 536) filled with ash, which dates to Stratum I, was found sunk into this surface.

Fig. 1. General view of Square K/10 illustrating three superimposed strata in the village. **1.** Stratum I wall from rectilinear house; **2.** Stratum II wall from a large courtyard; **3.** Stratum III wall in excellent state of preservation. This wall (Wall 223) was found with a preserved height of 2.1 m and length of ca. 3.5 m. Note the stone foundation and mudbrick superstructure. Location of geology samples is indicated by tags on the section wall in the back.

Area D

Excavations in the area helped to clarify the stratigraphic relationship between one of the largest upper building phase (Stratum I) rectangular buildings (No. 13, ca. 4 × 12 m) and several subterranean features observed in the deep trench excavated in 1987. Below building No. 13 was another large rectangular building dated to Stratum II; it ran underneath and perpendicular to the upper building (fig. 6). A collection of 14 painted pebbles (Locus 719), similar to those found at Abu Matar (Perrot 1955: 168–70, pl. 21), was on a floor associated with this Stratum II building (fig. 7). A number of subterranean storage pits were also associated with the Stratum II rectangular building in Area D.

The excavations in the northern part of the site revealed a clustering of storage pits in this portion of the village. Very few of the pits are associated

with Stratum I, but many are found in Stratum II. Limited exposures now indicate that Stratum III is clearly separated from the upper building phases by fill deposits and other evidence of abandonment.

GEOLOGY

Geological research in the 1988 season concentrated on the nature of the deposits at the site, which included both anthropogenic and geogenic sediments. The principal aims were to clarify the types of site-formation processes operative during the occupation phases and to better understand the origins of various stratigraphic units and features.

Samples collected from a variety of sediments and materials are being studied using micromorphological techniques that employ petrographic thin sections. Sections are prepared by first indurating the undisturbed sample with polyester resin

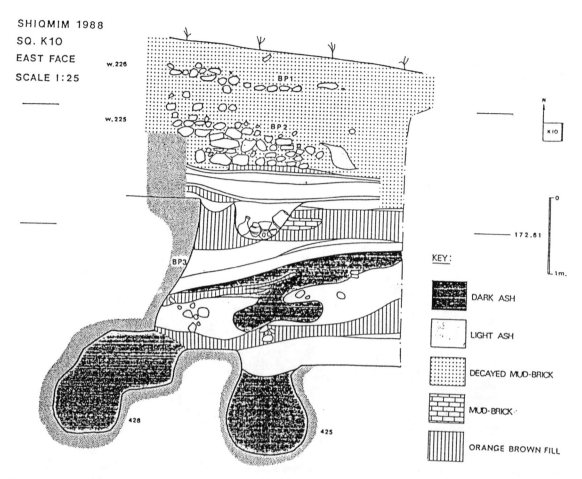

SHIQMIM 1988
SQ. K10
EAST FACE
SCALE 1:25

KEY:

■ DARK ASH

□ LIGHT ASH

▨ DECAYED MUD-BRICK

▤ MUD-BRICK

▥ ORANGE BROWN FILL

Fig. 2. Section drawing of eastern face of Square K/10. Note location of Pits Loci 425 and 428, which predate the construction of the Stratum I–III walls. In the center of the section, the cache (Locus 412) of pottery vessels sealed by a surface can be clearly seen.

under vacuum. The hardened block thus produced is then trimmed with a rock saw; the resulting slab is mounted on a glass slide and ground to the appropriate thickness (30 μ). Micromorphological analyses of thin sections permit a broad range of observations pertaining to composition, texture, and fabric of the material (see Courty *et al.* 1990 for details).

Some of the features, deposits, and materials sampled are discussed below.

• In Square H10, a 1 m thick lens of coarse silt/very fine sand, containing a few Byzantine sherds, could be traced from Square H11 south-southeast through Squares H9 and J9. This relatively large-scale feature seems to represent either a human-made or natural channel dug into the underlying Chalcolithic deposits. We anticipate that the micromorphological analyses will clarify it.

• Samples of mudbrick were taken to evaluate its composition and to determine its source. On the basis of field observations they appear made of the Upper Pleistocene silts and clays that constitute the base and northern back portion of the site.

• In many locations around the site we observed units of crudely and irregularly bedded decayed mudbrick interbedded with ash and irregular blotches of sterile silt. Samples were collected to evaluate the processes of mudbrick and wall decay. Particular emphasis was placed on fills located between standing mudbrick walls (fig. 1).

• Several layers containing ash, charcoal, and burnt material were sampled to determine the types of fuels used in different structures and strata throughout the site. Field observations indicated that different types of fuels were burned. Some ash layers contained wood charcoal, whereas others

Table 1. Basic Archaeozoological Data,
Shiqmim Faunal Collection, 1988

Species	Number of Bones and Teeth Identified	Proportionately Assigned
Sheep	85	700
Goat	71	585
Sheep/goat	754	0
Gazelle	21	31
Sheep/goat/gazelle	385	0
Cattle	85	172
Equid	5	10
Hartebeest	2	4
Large mammal	94	0
Pig	2	2
Dog	3	3
Fox	3	3
Lion	1	1
Bird	6	6
Ostrich	1	1
Hare	3	3
Totals	1521	1521

Fig. 3. Detail of two pits (Loci 425 and 428) provisionally assigned to Stratum IV, the earliest settlement phase at Shiqmim.

were rich in phytoliths, which suggest the burning of more grassy vegetation. Moreover, in certain cases the coarseness of the ash and associated burned material suggested that the material might be not from domestic waste but possibly from "industrial" activities such as pottery manufacture. The alternative working hypotheses can be readily checked with petrographic thin sections.

• A few samples were taken from an ash pit with alternating layers of medium gray and dark gray ash. We wished to clarify the function of such a pit filling and to explain the differences in ash types.

• Finally, samples of plaster were collected to obtain insights into how such materials might have been manufactured. Such knowledge will increase our understanding of the evolution of plaster technology from the Neolithic through the more recent historical periods in the Levant. Some of the ashy units described above may be related to the manufacture of these plasters.

ARCHAEOZOOLOGY:
THE VERTEBRATE REMAINS

A total of 2666 fragments of animal bones and teeth was recovered, of which 1048 (39 percent) have been identified to element and taxon. This suggests that fewer small fragments of bone were retrieved this season than in the 1987 season, when only 22 percent of the faunal remains could be identified.

In addition to those fragments, the very scanty remains of four sheep or goats were retrieved; three were very young lambs or kids (it has not been possible to identify their species), but the other is a sheep, whose dentition indicates that it belonged in Payne's age group C (ca. 6–12 months). The skeletons of the three younger animals were found in Area Y, Loci 434 (Baulk L 10/ L 11) and 432 (Baulk L 10/M 10), and that of the older one was in Area D, Locus 739 (Square 012). No other significant groups of animal bones were found.

The numbers of remains identified to taxon are shown in Table 1. As usual, many of the small ruminant bones could not be identified beyond the sheep/goat/gazelle or sheep/goat categories; these were allocated to the species counts in the same proportions as the bones that could be identified to species. Details of the methodology are in the

Fig. 4. Overview of pottery cache (Locus 412) sealed beneath Stratum 2 Wall 225.

Table 2. Domestic/Wild Proportions, Shiqmim Faunal Collection, 1988

Status and Species	Number
Domestic	
Sheep	700
Goat	585
Cattle	172
Dog	3
Total Domestic	1460
Percent Domestic	96
?Domestic	
Equid	10
Pig	2
Total ?Domestic	12
Percent ?Domestic	1
Wild	
Gazelle	31
Hartebeest	4
Fox	3
Lion	1
Bird	6
Ostrich	1
Hare	3
Total Wild	49
Percent Wild	3

Table 3. Domestic Ungulate Proportions, Shiqmim Faunal Collection, 1988

Species	Number	Percent	Number	Percent
Sheep	700	48		
Goat	585	40		
Sheep and Goats			1285	88
Cattle	172	12	172	12
Total	1457	100	1457	100

As with the material from previous seasons, the small size of the sheep, goat, and cattle bones shows that they are domestic; the canids from 1988 are also definitely of domestic dogs. The domestic status of the equid and pig bones is uncertain; however, together they constitute only 1 percent of the total sample. Because the remains of wild animals constitute only 3 percent of the total, it is clear that the animal-based part of the economy was overwhelmingly based on the husbandry of three domestic animals: sheep, goats, and cattle (see Table 2).

The relative numbers of the animals are shown in Table 3. As in 1987, sheep and goats make up 88 percent of the domestic ungulates and cattle 12 percent, and the bone definitely identified as sheep slightly outnumber those of goats. The two pig bones are fragmentary and come from immature animals; as they comprise less than 0.2 percent of the bones, they may be intrusive, possibly derived from wild animals, and of little or no economic,

interim report on the 1987 bones (Levy *et al.* 1990). A similar allocation was made with the large mammal bones, which were assigned to cattle, equids, and hartebeests in the same proportions as the bones definitely identified to those species.

Fig. 5. Two well-preserved Stratum II walls lining a semi-subterranean feature. At the bottom, a large bell-shaped pit is visible (Locus 515).

cultural, or environmental importance. As in Shiqmim, pigs are virtually absent from all the Chalcolithic sites in the Beersheva valley but are frequent in sites nearer to the Mediterranean.

Although few in number, the wild animal remains are of some interest. The foxes, the hare, and the hartebeest probably were eaten, but the lion is represented by a single foot bone that might have been brought to the site inside a pelt. It is not known when hartebeests became extinct in the Middle East, but their remains are quite common in the southern half of Israel until at least the Bronze Age. Ostrich egg shell fragments are common in the southern half of Israel until at least the Bronze Age. Ostrich egg shell fragments are common in archaeological sites in the Negev, but their bones are almost never present. If they were hunted, they were probably butchered where they fell and only the meat and feathers were brought back to habitation sites. The one ostrich bone found at Shiqmim is the distal end of a femur with cut marks, suggesting that the meat had been

stripped from the bone. The few other bird bones have not yet been identified to anatomical element or taxon.

INTRASITE VARIABILITY OF LITHIC TOOLS AND DEBITAGE

Analyses of chipped stone tools from Chalcolithic sites have focused primarily on total assemblages from a given site with little regard for temporal or spatial variability. While this level of analysis is an essential component of any site analysis, the potential exists for achieving greater understanding of intrasite spatial dynamics and activity areas through more detailed analyses. Intrasite spatial analyses of lithic tools and debitage may provide complementary indicators of activity areas and possible functions of differing areas within one site (cf. Hietala 1984).

Following Rosen (cf. Levy *et al.* 1990), loci excavated in 1988 were selected to represent the types of deposition and features characteristic of the Shiqmim village. Table 4 presents a locus list, with depositional character, volume, and summarized waste and tool counts. Table 5 indicates broad typological frequencies of debitage and tools by locus. Typological definitions follow those of Levy and Rosen (1987). As they have previously noted, four or five broad categories of raw material are recognizable, with all but one originating from the local wadi gravels. The exception is a very fine grained flint from which "tabular" fan scrapers were manufactured, possibly originating in the western Negev highlands (Rosen 1983).

Figure 8 presents the ratio of tools to debitage. Relatively clear clustering by depositional type is indicated for surfaces, pits, and hearths. Topsoil and fill loci, while somewhat distinct, are tightly clustered, suggesting that further tests are necessary to determine if this is statistically significant. A comprehensive study by Rowan (1990) has been made to determine the statistical correlates of all loci types with the lithic assemblage. Both fill and topsoil loci show relatively low tool and waste densities, as would be expected for areas unlikely to represent *in situ* areas of human activity. In the present analysis, high densities of waste and moderate to high tool densities, characteristic of pits, probably indicate use of the pit as waste receptacles, though this may be a secondary function. Surfaces show a high to moderate tool density, with a

Table 4. Summarized Contextual Data for Selected Loci from the
1988 Shiqmim Village Excavations

Locus	Volume	Stratum	Character	Tools		Waste	
				Total	Density	Total	Density
701	0.31	IIb	surface	12	38.7	60	193.5
708	0.82	IIb	surfaces	16	19.5	96	117.0
716	0.54	IIb	surfaces	32	13.0	26	48.1
2874	2.24	IIb	room floor	19	18.5	149	66.5
735	0.75	IIa	surface	8	10.7	49	65.3
720	0.18	IIa	surface	3	16.7	44	244.9
2892	0.55	IIb	pit	10	18.2	104	189.1
731	1.04	IIa	pit	33	31.7	233	224.0
372	0.20	I	hearth	2	10.0	53	265.0
564	0.05	II	surface	1	20.0	6	120.0
350	8.80	I	topsoil	8	0.9	9	1.0
509	4.48	I	topsoil	14	3.1	111	24.8
375	14.04	I/II	fill	17	1.2	219	15.6
351	2.88	I	topsoil	12	4.2	47	16.3
360	5.28	I	fill	1	0.2	20	3.8
505	5.12	I	topsoil	37	7.2	311	60.7
501	4.30	I	topsoil	14	3.3	124	28.8
506	6.06	I	fill	3	0.5	97	16.0
508	8.80	I	fill	21	2.4	157	17.8
512	0.62	I	room fill	81	6.5	77	124.2
513	1.60	I	fill	3	1.9	53	33.1
516	3.85	II	surface	14	3.6	75	19.5
531	0.48	II	surface	14	29.2	71	148.0
400	0.80	II	pit	8	10.0	257	321.3
713	1.10	II	pit	37	33.6	296	269.1
721/730	1.53	IIa/b	pit	57	37.3	516	337.3
744	1.20	IIb	pit	10	8.3	265	220.0
543	0.07	II?	hearth	0	0.0	5	71.4
544	0.10	II?	hearth	0	0.0	2	20.0
545	0.14	II	hearth	0	0.0	18	128.6
547	2.16	II	surface?	25	11.6	182	84.3
511	1.20	I	surface/fill	10	8.3	77	64.2

higher ratio of tools to waste than the other depositions and features, illustrating their work-related nature. Hearths characteristically have virtually no tools and moderate to low waste densities, indicating a lack of chipped stone tool use or waste disposal in their formation.

Future analysis will focus on differences between types of fills (silt, mudbrick, etc.), types of surfaces (courtyard, interior, exterior), and any correlations these finer distinctions may have with different occupational phases of the village. Preliminary observations support the thesis that comparative intrasite analyses of spatial patterning will provide useful insights into activity areas and depositional formations of Chalcolithic villages.

POTTERY

The 1988 excavation season produced an extraordinary quantity of pottery. A total of 1,074 kg of pottery was recovered and processed (sherds and complete vessels; Tables 6, 7). This quantity is almost equivalent in weight to the entire amount collected during the three seasons of excavation from 1982 to 1984, when 1,174.20 kg were processed (Levy and Holl 1987: 393; Table 6). There were two reasons for the increase. First, many more pits and subterranean features were discovered than in previous seasons. Preliminary observations show that underground facilities produce more pottery (complete, restorable, and fragmen-

Fig. 6. Area D, general view of Stratum I, Room 13 and earlier Stratum II room running beneath and perpendicular to this structure. Note the mudbrick superstructure of the earlier walls and, in the rear, the location of a collection of painted pebbles that has been left pedestaled at the Stratum II floor level (see arrow).

tary) than other types of loci at Shiqmim because of their use for storage and, secondarily, for trash disposal. Second, more than 40 complete shapes were found, including three caches of complete pottery vessels (Loci 412, 417, and 424).

The context of the caches is of key importance for reconstructing aspects of ritual behavior at Shiqmim. In the case of the cache in Locus 412 (figs. 2, 4, and 9) a pit was dug, then ten pottery vessels were placed carefully inside, and finally the pit was sealed by a surface over 5 cm thick. This cache included a fenestrated stand (B. 177), an imitation of examples made from basalt; two small globular jars covered in a white slip and brilliant red bands (B. 7178 and B. 7186); a jar with high flared neck and interior red flames, multiple handles, and geometric red triangles (B. 7179); a large deep basin (B. 7184); and four V-shaped bowls (B. 7180–B. 7183). Another cache (Locus 424; fig. 10) was found in the vicinity of Locus 412, with a sim-

ilar repertoire of vessels (fenestrated stand, high-neck jar, V-shaped bowls, hole-mouth jars). Pottery caches found previously at Shiqmim are related to offerings (cf. Levy 1987: 527). They have also been reported from other Chalcolithic sites, such as Bir es-Safadi (Commenge-Pellerin 1990: fig. 6) and Gerar (Gilead 1989: 382). Identifying the precise meaning of those caches, however, goes beyond the scope of this article.

Of the 51,966 sherds processed from this season, 69 percent were of coarse ware and 31 percent were of fine ware (Table 6). As part of the sherd analysis, the minimum number of pottery vessels represented by the ceramic assemblage was determined for each locus. Previous studies indicate that fine ware sherds are characteristic of V-shaped bowls and small hole mouth and globular jar vessels. Coarse wares are typical of the majority of ceramic types such as pithoi, hole mouth jars, jars, large bowls, basins, churns, and fenestrated stands (cf. Levy and

Table 5. Lithic Frequencies by Locus and Type, Shiqmim, 1988

	Topsoil					Fill						Surface/Floor										Pit							Hearth		
Locus	351	505	501	350	509	360	506	508	512	513	375	516	547	531	2874	701	716	735	720	564	511	731	400	713	730	7462	892	372	543	544	545
Chips	0	7	3	0	4	2	0	6	8	1	3	0	10	3	2	5	0	2	3	0	5	23	18	0	69	22	25	5	1	0	2
Chunks	15	160	51	3	41	3	47	64	33	12	79	32	45	28	45	15	9	17	3	3	35	57	72	50	127	64	59	25	1	1	14
Flakes	24	83	50	2	34	11	26	62	25	16	91	21	79	20	64	29	10	19	22	2	28	76	87	153	185	92	47	10	1	0	2
Primary flakes	3	35	12	3	18	1	17	15	7	13	21	13	24	13	20	6	2	6	5	1	6	35	51	57	57	59	11	8	1	1	0
Blades	3	12	6	0	5	1	5	9	3	7	17	6	15	6	15	3	3	5	8	0	3	28	25	24	63	19	8	2	1	0	0
Core trim.	1	10	1	1	2	0	1	0	0	3	0	2	1	0	1	0	0	0	2	0	0	9	1	8	9	4	2	3	0	0	0
Cores-flakes	1	4	1	0	6	2	1	1	1	1	6	1	6	1	2	1	1	0	1	1	0	4	0	4	4	5	2	0	0	0	0
Cores-blades	0	0	0	0	0	0	0	0	0	0	2	0	0	0	0	0	0	0	0	0	0	0	2	0	0	0	0	0	0	0	0
Cores-mix	0	0	0	0	1	0	0	0	0	0	0	0	2	0	0	0	1	0	0	0	0	1	0	0	2	0	0	0	0	0	0
Waste Total	47	311	124	9	111	20	97	157	77	53	219	75	182	71	149	60	26	49	44	6	77	233	257	296	516	265	104	53	5	2	18
Utilized primary flakes	1	1	1	0	1	1	0	0	0	0	0	1	3	0	0	0	0	2	0	0	0	4	0	3	5	1	0	0	0	0	0
Retouched/utilized flakes	7	21	7	4	8	0	1	12	0	3	14	3	8	4	11	4	2	1	2	2	6	14	2	12	24	5	1	0	0	0	0
Retouched/utilized blades	1	2	1	1	0	0	0	1	1	0	0	0	1	0	1	1	0	0	0	0	0	2	1	2	3	1	0	0	0	0	0
Sickles	2	2	0	1	0	0	0	1	0	0	1	1	1	0	0	3	0	0	0	0	0	1	1	0	1	0	2	0	0	0	0
Sickle blanks	0	2	0	0	0	0	1	0	0	0	0	0	2	5	0	0	0	0	0	0	0	1	0	0	0	0	0	0	0	0	0
Borers	0	2	0	0	0	0	0	1	0	0	0	0	0	0	1	0	0	0	0	0	1	0	0	0	0	0	1	0	0	0	0
Celts	0	0	0	1	0	0	0	0	0	0	0	0	0	1	1	0	0	0	0	0	0	0	0	0	0	0	0	0	0	0	0
Notches	0	1	0	0	1	0	0	0	0	0	0	0	0	0	0	0	0	0	0	0	0	1	0	2	0	0	1	0	0	0	0
Denticulates	0	1	0	0	1	0	0	0	0	0	0	1	3	1	2	0	0	1	0	0	0	1	0	1	1	1	1	0	0	0	0
Choppers	0	0	0	0	0	0	0	2	2	0	0	0	0	0	0	0	1	0	0	0	0	3	3	0	3	0	2	0	0	0	0
Scrapers	0	2	1	0	1	1	0	0	0	0	1	4	0	2	2	1	2	1	0	2	0	1	0	7	3	1	2	1	0	0	0
Hammerstone	0	0	0	0	0	0	0	0	0	0	0	0	0	0	0	0	0	0	0	0	0	0	0	0	0	0	0	0	0	0	0
Varia	0	0	0	0	0	0	0	1	0	0	1	1	0	0	0	0	0	0	0	0	0	0	0	0	0	0	0	0	0	0	0
Tab. scrapers	0	0	0	0	0	0	0	0	0	0	0	0	1	0	0	0	0	0	0	0	1	0	0	0	1	0	1	0	0	0	0
Intrusives	0	0	0	0	0	0	0	0	0	0	0	0	0	0	0	0	0	0	0	0	0	0	0	0	0	0	0	0	0	0	0
Misc. trim.	1	3	3	1	2	0	0	0	1	0	0	1	4	1	1	3	2	3	3	1	1	6	2	9	14	2	0	1	0	0	1
Tool Total	12	37	14	8	14	1	3	21	4	3	17	14	25	14	19	12	7	8	3	3	10	33	8	37	57	10	10	2			
Grand Total	59	348	138	17	125	21	100	178	81	56	236	89	46	85	168	72	32	57	47	7	87	266	265	333	573	275	114	55			

Table 6. Number and Percentage of Sherds per Stratum, by Ware and Vessel Part

Stratum/exposure (m²)	I 756.08		II 141.43		IIa 91.83		IIb 56.01		II total 289.27		III 30.59		Total 1075.94	
	No.	%	No.	%	No.	%	No.	%	No.	%	No.	%	No.	%
Coarse														
Rims	791	4	542	5	253	3	272	3	1067	4	49	6	1907	4
Bases	572	3	417	4	202	3	205	2	824	3	57	7	1453	3
Lugs	35	0	44	0	25	0	29	0	98	0	6	1	139	0
Body	14136	63	7046	64	4621	62	6177	59	17844	62	497	63	32477	62
Total	15534	70	8049	73	5101	69	6683	64	19833	69	609	77	35976	69
Fine														
Rims	1767	8	801	7	638	9	991	9	2430	8	54	7	4251	8
Bases	706	3	420	4	283	4	414	4	1117	4	36	5	1859	4
Lugs	7	0	5	0	3	0	8	0	16	0	1	0	24	0
Body	4263	19	1694	15	1417	19	2393	23	5504	19	89	11	9856	19
Total	6743	30	2920	27	2341	31	3806	36	9067	31	180	23	15990	31
Total sherds	22277	100	10969	100	7442	100	10489	100	28900	100	789	100	51966	100
Total weight (kg)	391.94		324.21		145.9		171.9		642.04		40.21		1074.19	

Table 7. Minimum Number and Percentage of Vessels per Stratum by Ceramic Type, 1988 Season

Stratum/ exposure (m²)	I 756.08		II 141.43		IIa 91.83		IIb 56.01		II total 289.27		III 30.59		Total 1075.94	
	No.	%	No.	%	No.	%	No.	%	No.	%	No.	%	No.	%
Pithoi	7	1	9	1	2	1	2	0	13	1	1	2	21	1
Hole-mouth (f)	20	2	26	4	17	5	22	5	65	5	4	7	89	4
Hole-mouth (c)	84	9	72	12	40	12	43	9	155	11	9	17	248	10
Globular jars	90	9	69	11	31	9	48	10	148	10	7	13	245	10
Jars	32	3	9	1	5	1	5	1	19	1	1	2	52	2
V-shaped bowls	472	48	267	44	170	49	252	53	689	48	21	39	1182	48
Bowls	102	10	47	8	25	7	38	8	110	8	1	2	213	9
Basins	151	15	96	16	50	14	53	11	199	14	7	13	357	15
Churns	14	1	11	2	5	1	7	1	23	2	1	2	38	2
Cornets	0	0	0	0	0	0	0	0	0	0	0	0	0	0
Fenestrated	3	0	3	0	0	0	0	0	3	0	1	2	7	0
Cups	0	0	0	0	0	0	2	0	2	0	0	0	2	0
Stoppers	0	0	0	0	0	0	0	0	0	0	0	0	0	0
Varia	1	0	2	0	0	0	0	0	2	0	1	2	4	0
Total	976	100	611	100	345	100	472	100	1428	100	54	100	2458	100

Menahem 1987). In the 1988 sample, the most common vessel type is V-shaped bowls. As seen in Table 7, 472 V-shaped bowls were found in Stratum I, 689 in Stratum II, and 21 in Stratum III, representing 48 percent of the typological assemblage in Stratum I and II and 39 percent in Stratum III (Table 7). The difference between Stratum III and the other strata can be accounted for by the smaller exposure of Stratum III deposits (Table 6). When the distribution of vessel types per stratum is examined by percentage (Table 7), little change is noticeable. This observation will be tested with a Chi-square statistic in the future. However, the interim results presented here highlight the difficulty of determining chronological change on the basis of pottery in the Beersheva Valley Chalcolithic culture.

One of the most interesting characteristics of this assemblage is the lack of any cornet vessels. Although they are common at sites on the Nahal Patish (Gilat) and Nahal Gerar (Alon and Levy 1989; Gilead 1989: 383), they are extremely rare in the Beersheva Valley sites. Not a single cornet sherd has been found at Shiqmim (Table 7, Levy and Menahem 1987). At Bir es-Safadi, Commenge-Pellerin (1990: 3) identified eight (0.03 percent) examples from a total of 22,736 sherds. At Gilat, an analysis of the 1987 ceramic assemblage showed a minimum of 644 vessels for all five strata, of which 35 (5.4 percent) were cornets. It is still not possible to clarify whether the differences are due to cultural and temporal factors.

CEMETERY EXCAVATIONS AND HUMAN SKELETAL REMAINS

During the 1988 season, five excavated areas contained burials. Three were within the Shiqmim cemetery complex northwest of the village, and two human burial loci were found within the village itself. Two new hilltops within the mortuary complex were explored in Cemeteries 5 and 6. In addition, a survey in the cemetery demonstrated that the extent of the mortuary site is larger than previously estimated. Whereas previous estimates suggested a length of ca. 800 m for the complex, the 1988 survey and excavation showed that mortuary structures extend for another 350–400 m along the north bank of the Nahal Beersheva to an area labeled Cemetery VII. The following report summarizes the results of the excavation and preliminary physical anthropology study of the mortuary installations that produced human remains.

Fig. 7. Detail of painted pebbles (Locus 719) found on the floor of the large rectangular building.

Cemetery V

This hilltop cemetery is ca. 250 m northwest of the village on one of the Eocene chalk hills along the north bank of the Nahal Beersheva. Like the other cemeteries at Shiqmim, Cemetery V consists of a cluster of mortuary structures that extend over the hilltop. An exposure of 500 m² (20, 5 × 5 meter squares) was opened in Cemetery V; 11 mortuary structures (primarily stone-lined circles) were discovered. Many of those structures were disturbed, and only three showed clear evidence of human bone remains. Structure 101 contained the best preserved human remains. Although no burial offerings were found there, more than 150 identifiable human bones were recovered. Compared with other Shiqmim cemeteries, the distribution of mortuary installations was not very dense in Cemetery V.

Structure 100. This structure is on the southernmost part of the hilltop overlooking the Nahal Beersheva. It has a maximum outside diameter of 2.90 m, an inside diameter of 1.95 m, and a maximum depth inside the circle of 0.80 m. The burials in it were disturbed; bones were found scattered all over the floor, with concentrations in the northeast and southern parts of the circle. Field observations indicated that the bones represent a secondary burial. They comprise the remains of two adults, one female aged 20 and the other aged 40. A subcircle of stones found inside Structure 100 contained two cranial fragments of a child. This type of interment suggests special burial treatment for this child. No gross pathology was noted in any of the bone samples from this structure.

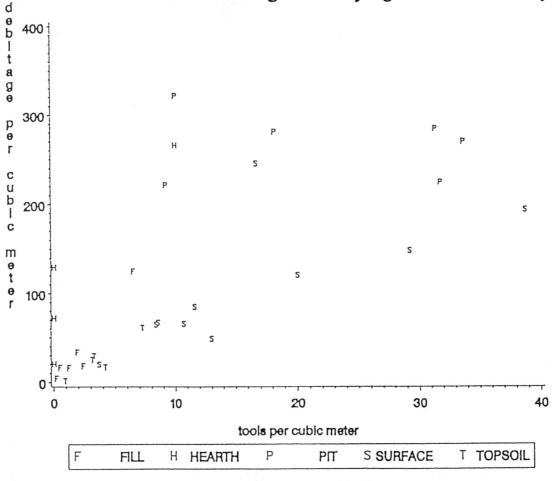

Fig. 8. Ratio of tools to waste, 1988 lithic assemblage.

Structure 101. Located north of Structure 100, this smaller circle has a maximum outside diameter of 1.70 m; an inside diameter of 1.40 m; and a maximum depth of 0.22 m. This circle was also disturbed and contained only a single grave good, a bead (Basket No. 5107). Human remains covered most of the floor (fig. 11). Along the western wall was a concentration of long bones lying parallel to each other. Their position suggests that those bones were stacked as part of a secondary burial. At least 12 individuals were identified from this grave circle, including seven children, three of whom are aged 3 to 4 years, two 7 years, one 8 to 9 years, and one 12 to

14 years. Of the five adults, one is estimated to have been 40 years old, based on the amount of attrition on the teeth; its sex was not determined. Two of the adults were female, one was male, and two were of undetermined sex. No ages could be determined for the remaining adult samples.

Cemetery VI

Cemetery VI is located within the Shiqmim mortuary complex, ca. 130 m northwest of Cemetery 3, which was excavated in 1982 (Levy and Alon 1985). The maximum elevation on this hill-

Fig. 9. Detail of pottery cache (Locus 412) found in a pit that was sealed by a surface. Note the herring-bone design on the rim of the fenestrated stand, imitating fenestrated stands of basalt.

Fig. 10. Detail of pottery cache (Locus 424) with fenestrated stand, high-necked jar, V-shaped bowls, and a hole mouth jar covered by a V-shaped bowl.

top is 187.92 m above mean sea level. Four full squares (5 × 5 m) and three half-squares were opened, providing a 112.5 m² exposure. Ten mortuary structures were found in this small excavation including two well-built stone-lined cists, seven stone-lined circles, and a small stone-built platform. The most impressive structures found there during the 1988 season were two stone-lined cists (fig. 12). Structure 207 had an outside length of 2.72 m, an outside width of ca. 1.23 m, and a depth of 0.59 m. Structure 209 had an outside length of 2.65 m, an outside width of 1.94 m, and a depth of 0.77 m.

The lack of cultural material found in this cluster of mortuary structures suggests several possibilities; including that they may have been constructed but never used; or that they may have been "symbolic" graves, i.e., prepared for the dead but never actually used as receptacles for bones. The latter interpretation is preferable, because a V-Shaped bowl was found in each of the cists (as in all of the cists found to date at Shiqmim; cf. Levy and Alon 1985), indicating an offering and ritual use of the area. Although all deposits were sieved from the mortuary structures, only a single bone fragment was found.

Table 8. Individuals Identified from the Different Excavation Areas
at Shiqmim, 1987–1988

Year	Location	Age Range								Total
		0–18		18–25		25–40		40+		
		No.	%	No.	%	No.	%	No.	%	
1988	Structure 100	2	50	1	25	0	0	1	25	4
1988	Structure 101	7	58	0	0	4	33	1	8	12
1988	Structure 300	2	40	1	20	1	20	1	20	5
1988	Village	2	50	1	25	1	25	0	0	4
1988	Total	13	52	3	12	6	24	3	12	25
1987	Structure 51	6	22	18	67	0	0	3	11	27

Fig. 11. Detail of secondary human burials found in a grave circle (Structure 101, Cemetery V).

Fig. 12. General view of Cemetery VI, Shiqmim cemetery. Two well-built cist structures (Structures 207-left; 209-right), oval in shape, can be seen in the foreground.

Cemetery VII

This year an additional area of mortuary-related installations was discovered at the Meẓad Aluf site, ca. 500 m northwest of the Meẓad Aluf Ottoman fort. One grave circle was excavated in this area. Unlike the more typical Shiqmim grave structures, it was made entirely of thin wadi cobbles

(fig. 13), similar to the type used in the painted cobble installation found in Area D. The rather poorly preserved human remains were placed in a secondary context on the cobble pavement. No burial offerings were found. Given the shallowness of this mortuary structure and the associated bones (ca. 5 cm below the surface), it is quite possible that it was robbed in antiquity.

Fig. 13. Structure 300, Cemetery VII, Shiqmim. The floor of this structure is made of smooth wadi cobbles similar to those used in the painted pebble installation found in Area D (see fig. 7).

Fig. 14. Detail of the skeleton of a two-year-old child found in a trash deposit (Locus 431) within the village. Cribra was noted on the orbits of this skull.

Village Burials

Human skeletal remains were recovered from two loci in the village.

Locus 431. This locus, 1 m west of Wall 227 and dated to Stratum II, is a rubbish dump. Its dimensions are ca. 1 × 3 m in area and 0.5 m in depth. In addition to burnt wadi cobbles, flint debitage and cores, some ceramic sherds, and animal bones, the cranial remains of a two-year-old child were found, including jaw fragments and teeth (fig. 14). Cribra was noted on the orbits.

Locus 437. This locus seems to represent an intentional secondary burial dating to Stratum II (fig. 15). It is roughly circular, with a diameter of ca. 0.90 m and a thickness of 0.35 m. The almost complete remains of an 18-month-old child were found, along with the fragmentary remains of two adults (one young and one old) and some animal bones. The adult remains included a left zygomatic, a left clavicle, a male sacrum, a right patella, vertebrae exhibiting morphological changes associated with arthritis, ribs, and a right upper second molar of a young adult. It has been noted that arthritis is common from the age of 35 in

Fig. 15. General view of secondary burials (Locus 437) found within the village. The almost complete remains of an 18-month-old child were found in association with two adults.

ancient populations, which would indicate that in addition to the young adult (represented by at least one tooth), there is another adult about 35 years of age.

The infant skeleton was placed in the center of a circle defined by the adult ribs (fig. 15). The infant skeleton is fairly complete although disarticulated, whereas the adult skeletons are represented by only a few disarticulated bones, although all of the bones that were found were in an excellent state of preservation. The fact that none of the adult bones were articulated suggests that both the adult and the child burials were secondary. Two of the infant bones were complete and could be measured: the right ulna is 8.5 cm in length, and the right radius is 7.8 cm in length. Both measurements are less than half a standard deviation greater than the mean for infants 0.5 to 1.5 years old (after Johnston 1962: table 2, quoted in Bass 1987). That corresponds very well with the age estimate of 18 months established from the dentition.

Pathology

The only pathologies found in the village burials were lipping on the vertebrae and the phalanges of the adult remains from Locus 437, resulting from arthritis, and a mild form of cribra on the orbits of the infant from Locus 431. This porous condition of the eye orbits has been associated with vitamin or iron deficiency (Nathan and Hass 1966; Stuart-Macadam 1987), leading us to conclude that

this infant probably had an inadequate diet. The dental pathologies included an abscess on a mandible fragment from Structure 101, a second molar tooth with a carious lesion at the mesial cemento-enamel junction (the young adult in Locus 437 from the village), and three cases of severe attrition (one each in Structures 100, 101, and 300). The amount of attrition observed on the teeth of the older individuals is comparable to that found at other Chalcolithic sites and is due to the abrasive diets of these populations (cf. Sabari and Smith in press; Smith 1989).

Comparison with Other Shiqmim Cemeteries

The condition of the bones from the cemeteries was very poor, although those from Structure 101 were in better condition than the others. There are two reasons for this: first the burials in the mortuary structures were disturbed in antiquity; and second, the burials in the cemeteries were extremely close to the surface, exposing the bones more directly to the elements. On the other hand, the village skeletons were discovered in loose sediment at a depth of over 2.5 m. Because of the poor preservation of the skeletons from the cemeteries excavated in 1988 we were unable to take any measurements.

The 1988 cemeteries differ from Cemetery II (Structure 51), excavated in 1987, in the number of specimens identified and in the condition of the bones. Bones of at least 27 individuals were recov-

Table 9. Ages of Children Excavated in 1988

Age	Number of Children
18 months	1
2 years	1
3 years	2
4 years	1
5 years	1
6 years	0
7 years	2
8–9 years	1
10–12 years	1
12–14 years	1
16 years	1
Total	12

ered from Structure 51. Six, or 22 percent, were less than 20 years old. By comparison, in each of the structures excavated in 1988 the number of in-dividuals was fewer (see Table 8) but the percentage of children was greater, ranging from 40 percent of the specimens identified in Structure 300 to 58 percent in Structure 101. In Structure 51, 11 percent of the individuals were over 40 years old. In the 1988 structures the percentage of people in that age bracket ranged from 0 in the village to 25 in Structure 100. The preservation of the skeletal material from Cemetery 2, Structure 51, was better than the condition of such material excavated from Cemeteries V, VI, and VII in 1988.

As is usual with Chalcolithic cemeteries, no newborns or very young infants were found in any of the burial areas excavated to date in the cemetery complex at Shiqmim (Table 9). This may be attributed to the poor reservation of the skeletal material, or to the fragile nature of infant bones. It seems more likely, however, that the bodies of newborns and young infants may have been handled differently than those of older children and adults (Smith 1989).

NOTE

[1]The 1988 season of excavation was carried out between 7 September and 14 October, 1988. This was the sixth excavation season and the second year of the Phase II multidisciplinary investigation, which focuses on the study of the earliest habitation layers at the site. The project was codirected by T. E. Levy (Principal Investigator) of the University of California, San Diego, and D. Alon of the Israel Antiquities Authority. The project was funded by the National Endowment for the Humanities (Grant No. 21541-87), grants from the Skirball Foundation, the C. Paul Johnson Family Charitable Foundation (Chicago) and several travel grants from the Anglo-Israel Archaeological Society. The expedition was sponsored by the Nelson Glueck School of Biblical Archaeology, Hebrew Union College, Jewish Institute of Religion, Jerusalem, and is affiliated with the American Schools of Oriental Research. For aid in the preparation of this report, we gratefully acknowledge the financial assistance of the Jerusalem Center for Anthropological Studies (JCAS) and in particular, its director, E. Siskin.

The core staff of the project included: J. Buikstra and P. Smith, physical anthropology; P. Goldberg, geology; G. Goodfriend, fossil land snail analyst; I. Carmi, isotope dating; M. Kislev, archaeobotany; C. Grigson, archaeozoology; A. Holl and T. E. Levy, anthropological archaeology; S. Shalev, metallurgical analyst; A. Rosen, phytolith analyst; S. Rosen, lithic consultant; Y. Rowan, lithic analyst and field supervisor; C. Peachey, P. Kopecz, B. O'donabain, and D. Gamill, field supervisors; F. Dillon and A. Jones, laboratory supervisors; I. Al-Assam, major domo; and A. Levy, administrator. A team of 14 workers from El Kom and Tel Sheva and 50 volunteers from Israel, Europe, and the United States participated in the excavation. We thank I. Sharon for his assistance in data processing.

BIBLIOGRAPHY

Alon, D., and Levy, T. E.
    1989   The Archaeology of Cult and the Chalcolithic Sanctuary at Gilat. *Journal of Mediterranean Archaeology* 2: 163–221.
Bass, W. M.
    1987   *Human Osteology. A Laboratory and Field Manual.* St. Louis: Missouri Archaeological Society.

Commenge-Pellerin, C.
    1990   *La Poterie De Safadi (Beersheva) au IVe Millenaire Avant L'ere Chretienne.* Paris: Association Paleorient.
Courty, M.-A.; Goldberg, P.; and Macphail, R.
    1990   *Soils and Micromorphology in Archaeology.* Cambridge: Cambridge University.

Gilead, I.
1989 Grar: A Chalcolithic Site in the Northern Negev, Israel. *Journal of Field Archaeology* 16: 377–94.

Hietala, H.
1984 Variations on a Categorical Data Theme: Local and Global Considerations with Near-Eastern Paleolithic Applications. Pp. 44–53 in *Intrasite Spatial Analysis in Archaeology*, ed. H. Hietala. Cambridge: Cambridge University.

Levy, T. E.
1987 *Shiqmim I. Studies Concerning Chalcolithic Societies in the Northern Negev Desert, Israel (1982–1984).* BAR International Series 356. Oxford: British Archaeological Reports.

Levy, T. E., and Alon, D.
1985 The Chalcolithic Mortuary Site Near Mezad Aluf, Northern Negev Desert: Third Preliminary Report, 1982 Season. *Bulletin of the American Schools of Oriental Research Supplement* 23: 121–35.

Levy, T. E., and Holl, A.
1987 Theory and Practice in Household Archaeology: A Case Study from the Chalcolithic Village at Shiqmim. Pp. 373–418 in *Shiqmim I*, ed. T. E. Levy. BAR International Series 356. Oxford: British Archaeological Reports.

Levy, T. E., and Menahem, N.
1987 The Ceramic Industry at Shiqmim: Typological and Spatial Considerations. Pp. 313–31 in *Shiqmim I*, ed. T. E. Levy. BAR International Series 356. Oxford: British Archaeological Reports.

Levy, T. E., and Rosen, S.
1987 The Chipped Stone Industry at Shiqmim: Typological Considerations. Pp. 281–94 in *Shiqmim I*, ed. T. Levy. BAR International Reports 356. Oxford: British Archaeological Reports.

Levy, T. E.; Alon, D.; Goldberg, P.; Grigson, C.; Smith, P.; Buikstra, J. E.; Holl, A.; Rosen, S. A.; Shalev, S.; Ben Itzhak, S.; and Ben Yosef, A.
1990 Protohistoric Investigations at the Shiqmim Chalcolithic Village and Cemetery: Interim Report on the 1987 Season. *Bulletin of the American Schools of Oriental Research Supplement* 27: 29–46.

Nathan, H., and Haas, N.
1966 "Cribra Orbitalia." A Bone Condition of the Orbit of Unknown Nature. *Israel Journal of Medical Sciences* 2: 171–91.

Perrot, J.
1955 The Excavations at Tell Abu Matar, near Beersheba. *Israel Exploration Journal* 5: 17–41, 73–84, 167–89.
1984 Structures d'habitat, mode de vie et environment: les villages, souterrains des pasteurs de Beershéva dans le Sud d'Israël, au IVe millénaire avant l'ère chrétienne. *Paléorient* 10: 75–96.

Rosen, S.
1983 Tabular Scraper Trade: A Model of Material Culture Dispersion. *Bulletin of the American Schools of Oriental Research* 249: 79–86.

Rowan, Y.
1990 A Chalcolithic Chipped Stone Assemblage from the Northern Negev Desert: Phase II (1987–1989) Investigations at Shiqmim. Unpublished M.A. thesis, University of Texas (Austin).

Sabari, P., and Smith, P.
In Press The Chalcolithic Skeletal Remains from Horvat Hor. ʿAtiqot.

Smith, P.
1989 The Skeletal Biology and Paleopathology of Early Bronze Age Populations in the Levant. Pp. 297–316 in *L'urbanisation de la Palestine à l'âge de Bronze ancien: Bilan et perspectives de recherches actuelles*, ed. P. de Miroschedji. BAR International Series 527. Oxford: British Archaeological Reports.

Stuart-Macadam, P.
1987 Porotic Hyperostosis: New Evidence to Support the Anemia Theory. *American Journal of Physical Anthropology* 74: 521–26.

The Neolithic Village of ᶜAin Ghazal, Jordan: Preliminary Report on the 1989 Season

GARY O. ROLLEFSON
Department of Anthropology
San Diego State University
San Diego, CA 92182

ZEIDAN KAFAFI
Institute of Archaeology and Anthropology
Yarmouk University
Irbid, Jordan

ALAN H. SIMMONS
Desert Research Institute
University of Nevada System
Reno, NV 89506

The sixth season of excavations continued work in the South and Central Fields of the site, and exploratory trenches sampled the previously untested North and West Fields. Substantial Late PPNB (ca. 6500–6000 B.C.) architecture was exposed for the first time. A better understanding of the site's history was gained, including information pertaining to the transitions from the LPPNB to the PPNC and from the PPNC to the Yarmoukian periods. Twenty-three new burials were found, most of which date to the PPNC.

INTRODUCTION

In 1987 we learned that at least 90 percent of the Neolithic site of ᶜAin Ghazal was scheduled to be destroyed as part of the Municipality of ᶜAmman's commercial and residential development plan for northern and eastern ᶜAmman. Funds were raised for two seasons of emergency excavations at ᶜAin Ghazal to obtain as much information as possible from those portions of the site that were due to be destroyed.[1] In 1988 field work concentrated on the poorly explored Pre-Pottery Neolithic C (PPNC) and Yarmoukian deposits, expanding earlier, relatively small exposures of those cultural periods in the South and Central Fields (Rollefson, Kafafi, and Simmons 1990). The goals for the 1989 season continued to stress the investigation of the PPNC and Yarmoukian periods, as well as the sampling of deposits in the previously untested northern and western areas of the site, which held promise for revealing Late PPNB evidence that had not been abundantly exposed in earlier seasons. Two specific features also were examined for possible relevance to the Neolithic occupation of ᶜAin Ghazal: a small, square, walled structure that incorporated enormous stone blocks in its construction; and a cave in an exposed outcrop of limestone.

More than 350 m² and 200 m³ of cultural deposits were investigated during seven weeks of excavations at ᶜAin Ghazal in June and July 1989; an impressive array of economic, architectural, artifactual, and technological information was acquired in this sixth excavation season. Although it is a tragedy that this remarkable site will be sacrificed to "progress," we have managed to obtain at least a basic idea of the developments that unfolded over the two millennia history of this important settlement.

EXCAVATION AND SITE STRATIGRAPHY

The site map (fig. 1) displays the areas excavated in 1989. Clear evidence of transitions from the Late PPNB (LPPNB) to the PPNC and from the PPNC to the Yarmoukian period were found in all but two excavated areas; the exceptions were the

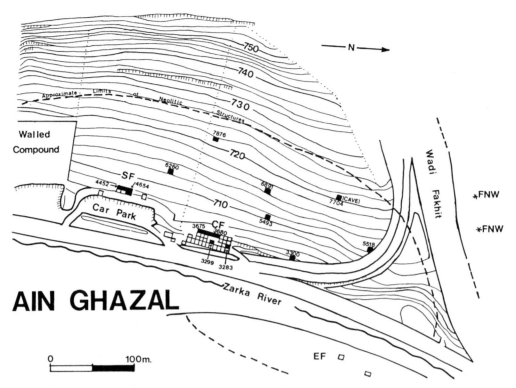

Fig. 1. Site map of ᶜAin Ghazal showing the 1989 excavation trenches (in black) in relation to earlier excavations (open squares; drawing by R. Baron).

stone-block structure in Square 7876 and the cave (Square 7704).

The Stone-Block Structure (Square 7876)

A large (ca. 5 × 5 m) square structure made of large (ca. 70 × 40 × 30 cm) blocks of limestone was situated near the westernmost (uphill) limit of the site. Only the very top of one course of the walls was visible in the northeast, southeast, and southwest corners of the structure; and the enclosed space was filled in with field stones and dirt, evidently the result of recent field clearing and slope erosion. An east-west trench 50 cm on either side of the walls in the northeast corner produced abundant potsherds beneath the overburden of the 20th-century stone pile, and the ceramics were principally Byzantine, with smaller amounts of Early Islamic sherds. The ceramic evidence stopped abruptly at the base of the walls, and "subfloor" excavation on both sides of the walls to a depth of ca. 25 cm produced only rolled chipped stone artifacts of indeterminate age.

It appears that the structure was an outbuilding constructed in late Byzantine times and that it may

have continued in use during the Early Islamic period. Certainly nothing indicates that the building had any relationship with the Neolithic populations of ᶜAin Ghazal. Other evidence supporting the same interpretation includes the remnant of a small Byzantine farmstead or field house on the extreme southern edge of ᶜAin Ghazal and, at the top of the hill some 150 m west of the structure, clear indications of a small Umayyad settlement (including a cistern) destroyed by new housing constructed in the mid-1980s.

The Cave (Square 7704)

A small opening visible in a limestone outcrop near the northwestern limits of the site suggested the presence of a cave that had been filled sometime during the occupation of ᶜAin Ghazal. The use of caves in ritual contexts during the Neolithic period in the Near East, as reflected by the spectacular contents of Nahal Hemar in southern Palestine (Bar-Yosef and Alon 1988), demanded that we investigate the deposits within this geological feature.

Excavation in the northern half of the cave revealed that the carstic cavity extended some 7 m into the hillside and narrowed to a rounded back wall from an opening approximately 4 m wide at the base of the cave mouth. Deposits inside the cave (deepest at the mouth) accumulated to a depth of 1.7 m.

The results of the excavation were disappointing, for metal, leather, plastic, and beer bottle sherds at the bottom of the deposits confirmed that the cave had been pot-hunted within the past several decades.

The cave was apparently used as a Byzantine crypt, for a relatively small rectangular chamber had been cut into the soft limestone bedrock, and at least one recessed ledge had been chipped into the northern cave wall. Scattered human bones (mostly a few phalanges and rib fragments) were found in the disturbed cave fill, as well as a small quantity of minute fragments of ribbed potsherds typical of Byzantine manufacture. It is evident that this episode of Byzantine use had destroyed earlier deposits in the cave from the Neolithic period (but no subsequent cultural periods), for chipped stone artifacts characteristic of both the Aceramic and Ceramic Neolithic were mixed with the human bones, pottery, and modern debris.

The Central Field

Six 5 × 5 m trenches were opened in the Central Field to connect Sectors I and II of the 1988 season (cf. Rollefson, Kafafi, and Simmons 1990: fig. 1) in an effort to expose as broad an area of Yarmoukian occupation in that part of the site as was possible under the constraints of the excavation schedule. While the emphasis was on Yarmoukian architecture and other material culture remains, PPNC layers were also reached in most of the trenches, and several more loci of PPNC/Yarmoukian transitional deposits appear to be represented among the sampled sediments. A striking example of the reuse of a PPNC structure by later Yarmoukian occupants was found fortuituously during the 1989 season in a 1988 excavation trench (Square 3483). Covered by plastic at the close of the 1988 season, a mud plaster floor had dried out in the intervening 12 months, and at the limits of the earlier excavations the floor had "exfoliated," showing clear evidence of a puddled-mud resurfacing (Yarmoukian) of two earlier episodes of PPNC flooring and reflooring separated by a thin veneer of red ochre paint.[2]

Square 3283 at the northeastern end of the Central Field array was also probed in an attempt to locate surfaces that may have been associated with the Yarmoukian apsidal building exposed in 1985 and 1988, as well as surfaces connected with the Yarmoukian reuse of the PPNC structure in Square 3483. Because of the contours of this part of the site's upper terrace and the intensive agricultural disturbance since the 1950s, no intact surfaces were encountered.

In addition, a burial, probably dating to the LPPNB, was excavated from the bulldozer section in Square 3279. Finally, the massive "courtyard wall" exposed in 1988 was sectioned in Square 3475 to obtain a clearer picture of the history of this feature.

The South Field

Work continued in and around several trenches of the 1984 and 1988 seasons to gain a more comprehensive understanding of the architecture and associated cultural material in this part of the site. The effort resulted in the virtually complete exposure of two PPNC house plans. Both house plans, each representing a successive phase of the PPNC, are very similar, although one entryway opens to the south, the other to the east. Both are also strongly similar to the Level II dwellings at Beidha, which Kirkbride (1966) has assigned to the middle of the seventh millennium B.C.[3]

The Exploratory Trenches

Although we knew before the beginning of the 1988 season at CAin Ghazal that an enormous portion of the site would be destroyed, it was never clear what parts might be preserved for future research. Indeed, after a series of negotiations with the Mayor of CAmman that produced "understandings" of the size and location of the portion to be preserved, critical areas of the "core area" of CAin Ghazal appear to be threatened at this time (Dornemann, personal communication).

Under the prevailing conditions of communication, "understandings," and economic pressures within Jordan, it was clear that random or stratified random sampling procedures could not be used for either the 1988 or the 1989 seasons. The frustrations encountered in the 1988 and early 1989 seasons made it obvious that traditional sampling techniques would have to be replaced by opportunistic choices entailing both visible and suspected areas of rational "promise."

The work in the 1982–1985 seasons was concentrated in the eastern (downhill) parts of the

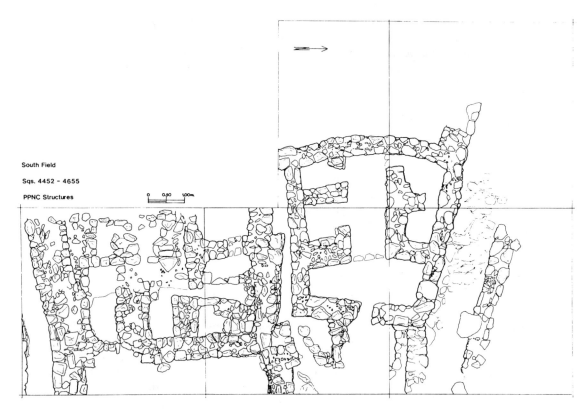

Fig. 2. Floor plans of PPNC structures in the South Field. The structure on the right, with an adjacent flagstone passageway and courtyard wall, has a narrow opening through a porch addition to the east. The slightly earlier structure to the left had a doorway in the center of the south wall (drawing by M. Dahash and R. Baron).

South and Central Fields, a circumstance governed by the exposure of threatened cultural materials in the bulldozer sections from the 1974/1981 highway construction project. A series of test trenches in 1983 revealed that probable PPNB architecture (red burnished plaster floor fragments) extended at least 160 m up the hill from the highway (Rollefson and Simmons 1985: 35), but subsequent investigation on a larger scale was not possible because of the pressures of work at lower elevations of the site.

Three 5 × 5 m trenches (Squares 6260, 6891, 5493; cf. fig. 1) were selected in the uphill parts of ᶜAin Ghazal because of their association with terraces that may have been either natural or cultural formations. In addition, two other trenches (Squares 3300 and 5518) were selected at the northern and northeastern edges of the main site area because of evidence exposed in the bulldozer sections.

The cultural phasing in all five trenches remains to be fine-tuned, but at the present state of analysis it appears that in addition to expanding the area of PPNC and Yarmoukian occupation, the excavation exposed major LPPNB (ca. 6500–6000 B.C.) archi-

tecture for the first time. We consider LPPNB, LPPNB/PPNC transitional, and PPNC deposits to be present in Squares 3300, 5518, and 5493. In Squares 6260 and 6891 the phase sequence runs unbroken from LPPNB through the PPNC through at least the early Yarmoukian period.

ARCHITECTURE

Central Field, Yarmoukian

At least three and perhaps four phases of Yarmoukian occupation have been identified in the Central Field, but only the earliest two produced definite traces of permanent architecture in 1989; the second phase obscured much of the construction detail of the earliest one. Isolated wall stubs and scattered stone alignments in the two latest phases may indicate that substantial construction once existed but was severely disturbed by mid-20th century plowing. It is also possible that those architectural remnants reflect instead elements of temporary structures, a condition that was confirmed in the 1985 season (Rollefson and Simmons

Fig. 3. The broad PPNC courtyard wall in the center was modified during the Yarmoukian period. The narrower wall to the left (north) is a later Yarmoukian courtyard wall (photograph by L. Rolston).

1987: 105) near the northern end of the Central Field.

Little architectural information was obtained for the earliest Yarmoukian phase, although it was clear that only that phase was associated with the massive stone "courtyard wall" uncovered in 1988 (Rollefson, Kafafi, and Simmons 1990). By partially dismantling this wall, we hoped to clarify its construction and use. Work in 1989 confirmed that the wall was originally constructed in the PPNC period and that it probably separated two plastered courtyards. In this regard, the PPNC wall has additional parallels with Phase II at Beidha (Kirkbride 1966: 14, fig. 2).

The wall was modified at least once during the PPNC/Yarmoukian transitional phase of occupation by the creation of an opening through it just east of Square 3675; this "gate" (if that is what it was) eventually was closed sometime during the earliest Yarmoukian phase, and the height of the wall was increased by at least one course of stones. The Yarmoukian modification is clearly delineated, for the single added course—all that remained by the second phase of the Yarmoukian—is narrower than the original PPNC wall by the width of a single row of stones on both sides (fig. 2).

Squares 3676 and 3677 revealed part of a second-phase Yarmoukian courtyard, including an exterior stone bench attached to the enclosure wall (fig. 2) and a geometric pattern of exterior postholes suggesting a "ramada"-like structure that would have provided a shaded work area open to breezes and indirect sunlight.

Although PPNC layers were reached throughout the Central Field, little indication of preserved PPNC architecture was encountered during the 1989 season. This is understandable in view of the tendency of the PPNC/Yarmoukian transitional and early Yarmoukian inhabitants of ᶜAin Ghazal to modify, sometimes extensively, earlier standing PPNC structures.

South Field-PPNC

In 1989 we exposed the complete floor plan and adjacent outdoor areas of a PPNC house only partially exposed in the 1984 and 1988 seasons (fig. 3). The parallels with Beidha Level II architecture could not be closer (cf. Kirkbride 1966: fig. 2), including a small paved passage outside the northern wall and what is probably a courtyard wall north of that walkway.

The house appears to have been used for a considerable period, reusing an earlier PPNB plaster floor. That suggests that it may have been a semi-subterranean structure. One of the interior PPNC walls partially covered a typical MPPNB circular floor hearth (cf. Rollefson and Simmons 1986: fig. 9). Since we have not found hearths in any of the LPPNB structures so far, we cannot rely on this use of a PPNB floor by PPNC architects as evidence of a PPNB-PPNC transition. The presence of a few undecorated potsherds beneath the abutting "porch walls" outside the entry on the eastern end of the building (Rollefson, Kafafi, and Simmons 1990) indicates that it was still in use

South Field

Sq. 6260

LPPNB/PPNC Structure

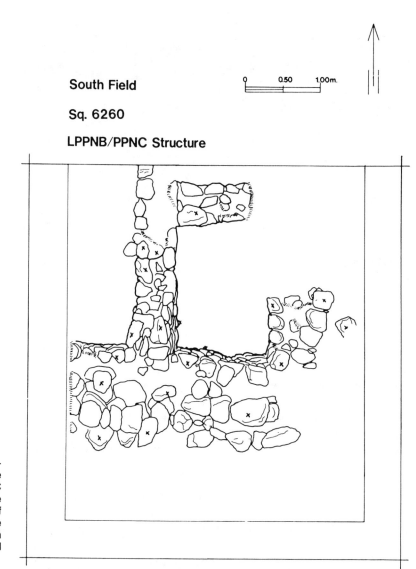

Fig. 4. Top plan of a badly damaged LPPNB house in Square 6260, remodeled in the PPNC and Yarmoukian periods. The walls in the Southwest corner of the small square chamber are preserved to a height of 1.62 m (drawing by M. Dahash and R. Baron).

during the PPNC/Yarmoukian transitional phase and perhaps even into the earliest Yarmoukian phase.

The dwelling in Squares 4455 and 4655 underwent several phases of renovation and modification. One phase included the closure of the northwest "cell," after this small room and the adjacent chamber to the east were converted to a burial crypt; there is no indication that the adjoining north-central roomlet ever opened onto the central corridor. The subfloor burial in the northwest cell, with the skull intact with the rest of the skeleton (as is typical for the PPNC period), cut through the PPNB floor, but the surface above the pit fill was never replastered. Other human bones

were scattered in this and the adjoining room, but they may have been intrusive after the house was abandoned in the PPNC/Yarmoukian transitional period or shortly thereafter. The south-central chamber also saw use as a special burial chamber, for a robust male skull complete with mandible was found on the floor there; on the other hand, the entrance to the chamber was not closed.

Immediately south of this PPNC house, work in 1989 completed the exposure of the floor plan of another, earlier PPNC house in Squares 4452–4453, first investigated in 1984 and 1988. Although certain details set it apart from its later neighbor to the north, the overall arrangement of cellular rooms is remarkably similar. (Fig. 3

Fig. 5. View of the building in fig. 4, to the west. The threshold of the entrance to the back chamber is ca. 60 cm above the base of the wall (photograph by L. Rolston).

records the final top plan after excavation through the floors in the eastern suite of rooms, after removal of some of the interior walls). One clear difference is that the entry to the southern house was from the south, not the east; another distinction is that all of the chambers opened onto a central north-south corridor. The subfloor "channel" found beneath the northeast chamber in 1988 (Rollefson, Kafafi, and Simmons 1990) appears to have been unique; no other subfloor channels were found in the building. This indicates that the suggested parallel of the "channeled buildings" in Area A in Basta (Nissen *et al.* 1987; cf. Rollefson, Kafafi, and Simmons 1990) was premature.

The Exploratory Trenches

Square 6260. Recent deep terracing and plowing severely disturbed one or more Yarmoukian structures in Square 6260 in the South Field; and while no clear plans could be distinguished for the latest occupations, the fragmented wall stubs suggest that pottery-using families modified and maintained earlier Aceramic Neolithic structures. One partially preserved structure in Square 6260 is particularly interesting (fig. 4). Only the far southwest small chamber and the southern wall of the adjoining eastern room survived the plowing, but the walls are preserved to a height of more than 1.5 m in some places (fig. 5). Because of the geometry of the southwest room, the structure appears to be a dwelling originally built in the LPPNB, modified considerably during the PPNC, and then reused by Yarmoukian inhabitants.

Projections of the minimum size of the rooms based on floor area and wall height in the LPPNB correlate well with the LPPNB structure excavated in Square 5518 (see below) and with the Basta PPNB structures (Nissen *et al.* 1987: figs. 6, 7), including a connecting passageway between the southwest adjacent room across a threshold some 60 cm above the bottom of the wall. The PPNC occupants evidently filled in the chambers so that the walls extended only a meter or so above the fill surface; it resembles the arrangement in the two houses in the eastern (downhill) section of the South Field. The presence of substantial quantities of decorated Yarmoukian potsherds above the PPNC surface, well below the tops of the walls, reflects continued use of the structure in the Ceramic Neolithic period.

Square 6891. Although this trench also suffered severely from agricultural disturbance in the uppermost levels, the southeast corner of a Yarmoukian house and an associated courtyard wall were uncovered; they enclosed a partially preserved flagstone pavement in which an *in situ* pot base was resting in a small fireplace. No clear evidence of Aceramic Neolithic structures was recovered, but both PPNC and PPNB (M?/L?) deposits were found beneath the pottery-bearing layers.

Square 5493. The terrace selected for investigation in this part of ᶜAin Ghazal was quickly (and frustratingly) shown to be of recent origin, associated with bulldozing sometime in the past several decades: the upper 1.5 m of sediments contained

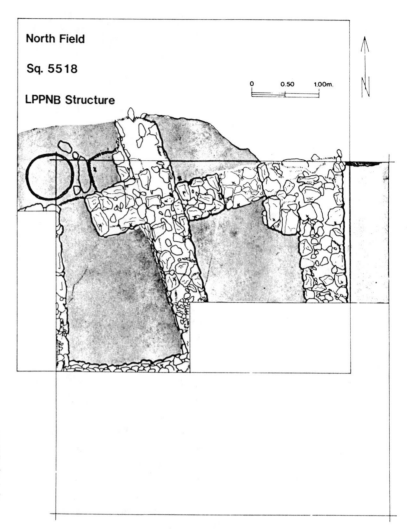

Fig. 6. Top plan of the LPPNB structure in Square 5518; stippling indicates the preserved extent of the lime plaster floor. The circular object to the upper left is a sun-dried clay vessel (drawing by M. Dahash and R. Baron).

such items as modern glass, leather, and metal objects. Uncontaminated levels were finally reached, but only mere stubs of walls were found, probably of PPNC date. Beneath those badly disturbed structural remnants, however, 15–25 cm of sediment covered limestone bedrock, into which was cut a large bedrock mortar with a series of cobbled steps that approached it from below. The associated chipped stone artifacts suggest tenuously that this feature is LPPNB in date, although it is not inconceivable that it may be MPPNB. Soil samples collected from the mortar depression have not yet been analyzed.

Square 5518. The road cut at the northern edge of ᶜAin Ghazal revealed a red painted plaster floor on cobble bedding just above the limestone base of the slope. Excavations in the trench produced no *in situ* evidence of Yarmoukian occupation, although

such evidence was probably destroyed by the bulldozing in this area that created farmable terraces long before road construction was initiated.[4] A thin veneer of sediments, on the other hand, has been assigned to the PPNC, although the evidence is weak for several of the loci—they may simply be LPPNB, in view of the sampling problems associated with so small an exposure.

Certainly the preserved architecture beneath the undisturbed upper layers must be ascribed to the LPPNB (fig. 6), for it mirrors many of the details of the LPPNB structures at Basta (Nissen *et al.* 1987) and contrasts sharply with MPPNB dwellings exposed in earlier seasons at ᶜAin Ghazal (e.g., Rollefson and Simmons 1986: figs. 7, 8). Walls were preserved to more than 1 m in height, despite the bulldozing, and rooms were subsquare but small, a bit less than 2 m on a side. Doors connected adjoining rooms, usually across a threshold ca. 15–20 cm

Fig. 7. View of the Square 5518 LPPNB house, to the south, showing the blocked doorway in the partition wall (photograph by L. Rolston).

Fig. 8. Large sun-dried clay storage vessel on the floor, partly blocking the doorway in the Square 5518 LPPNB house (photograph by L. Rolston).

above the floors. The floors were made of high quality lime plaster, covered with a rather thick application of red ochre; the joins of the walls and floors exhibited a characteristic "bathtub" contour. Much of the structure was destroyed during the road-cut bulldozing, but of the preserved portions, it can be stated unequivocally that some rooms did not have hearths built into the floors.

At one time, at least, the southwest room was used to store the harvest of legumes, for hundreds of charred peas and lentils were recovered from the floor surface.[5] Evidently a conflagration destroyed the contents of the room as well as the roof, for there was a considerable amount of burned clay covering, and in some areas it was mixed with, the underlying layer of charred pulses. The western wall appears to have been breached, for the pulse and clay layer is covered with an evident collapse of the relatively thin stone wall. There was no evidence of collapsed wall plaster mixed with the fill of the room, which contrasts with the evidence of typi-

cal wall finishing noted for the MPPNB in the Central Field (cf., Rollefson and Simmons 1988: 396).

The doorway leading to the adjacent eastern room was blocked (fig. 7), probably after the fire, although the entry to the northern room was left open. The stones blocking the doorway define a passage along the southern wall, ending at a threshold ca. 20 cm above the floor.

The doorway between the southwest room and the room to the north was evidently rarely used, for a large sun-dried clay storage vessel was placed on the floor just in front of the doorway, effectively blocking communication between the two rooms (fig. 8). The asymmetrical clay pot was preserved to a height of ca. 60 cm, and its diameter ranged from 60 to 70 cm. The pot was clearly placed in its position while the southwest room served as a storage room, for the fire that destroyed this room, charring the legumes in the process, also "fired" the clay vessel on the side that faced the doorway.

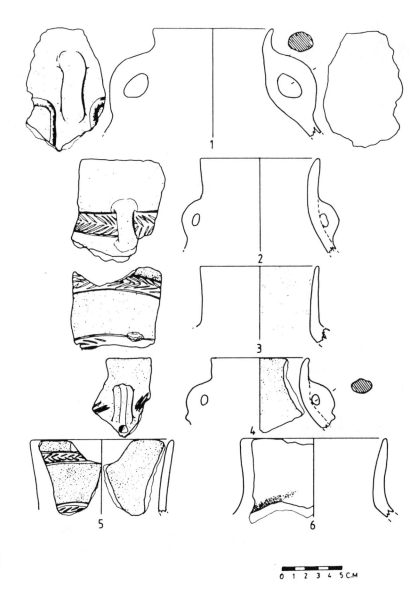

Fig. 9. Yarmoukian pottery vessels from the 1989 ᶜAin Ghazal season (drawing by A. Obeidat).

0 1 2 3 4 5 C.M

Square 3300. A thin, disturbed surface layer with Yarmoukian and later ceramics covered more than 2 m of aceramic deposits. The trench exposed the corner of a PPNC house that appears to have had one or more subfloor channels. Beneath the structure was a sequence of heavily damaged plaster floors and tumbled wall fragments, so badly disturbed during the Neolithic that no clear plans could be determined. At the bottom of the trench were two phases of plaster flooring, each severely damaged after abandonment when walls associated with the floors were completely robbed out. Highway construction added to the problems of interpretation, for only a strip of floors some 60–90 cm wide re-

mained in the section. Based on the few square meters that were preserved, the floor dimensions are more similar to the MPPNB examples than, for example, the LPPNB house floors in Square 5518.

Attempts to seriate the deposits between the MPPNB floors and the PPNC structure at the top of the section on the basis of lithic technology and typology were severely hampered by dense deposits of debitage associated with one or more chipping floors in Square 3300. More detailed analysis than has been possible so far may provide a better resolution of the LPPNB and PPNC layers, and dense accumulations of charcoal should help to define the temporal sequence in this trench.

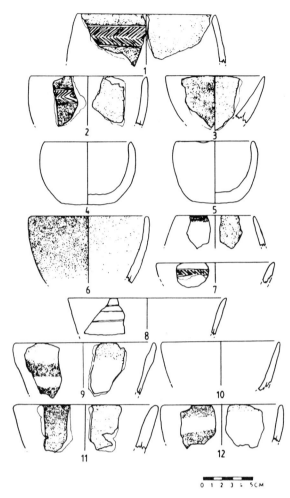

Fig. 10. Yarmoukian bowls from the 1989 ᶜAin Ghazal season (drawing by A. Obeidat).

POTTERY

The ceramic samples from the 1989 season were restricted for the most part to the Central Field trenches, although significant ceramic-bearing layers were also found in Squares 6260 and 6891. Elsewhere, uncontaminated pottery samples were isolated and generally confined to the uppermost portion of the depositional sequence.

As was the case in the 1988 season, potsherd densities were never particularly great in the Yarmoukian layers, at least compared, for example, to the Bronze and Iron Ages in the Near East. This suggests the presence of a "cottage industry," consistent with the emergence of local, small-scale ceramic production.

The repertoire of vessel forms was increased in the 1989 season by the addition of kraters, while

several new handles and the presence of ring bases marked a broader variation in styles than had been documented previously for the Yarmoukian period at ᶜAin Ghazal (figs. 9, 10). Bearing in mind the singular nature of the evidence, it is possible that one sherd from a Yarmoukian locus relatively high in the sequence of the Central Field may be from a bow-rimmed jar, tentatively attesting a very late Yarmoukian/PNB presence at ᶜAin Ghazal.

Based on the preliminary stratigraphic phasing of the 1988 and 1989 seasons, there is some basis for distinguishing "early" vs. "late" Yarmoukian pottery phases on the basis of decoration. After the appearance of undecorated crude ware of the PPNC/Yarmoukian transitional period, found in limited quantities in the 1988 and 1989 seasons, "true" Yarmoukian pottery may be signaled by the addition of red paint or red slip, followed by a later phase when incision of chevrons in a cartouche or as a banded herringbone design occurs either as a single design element or, more frequently, in combination with fields of red paint or slip. It must be stressed that this sequence is very tenuous at present. Much more detailed microstratigraphic comparisons must be done before any confidence can be assigned to this pattern.

CHIPPED STONE ARTIFACTS[6]

It has long been recognized that both typological and technological aspects of chipped stone tools and debitage are vital to distinguishing prehistoric periods of cultural development. That is particularly true for prehistoric archaeological surveys, when architectural, faunal, and botanical remains, and even pottery may not be visible among scatters of chipped stone artifacts exposed on the surface. The situation becomes critical for the Neolithic period in the Levant, for subtle but real changes took place in lithic production. A recent doctoral dissertation that examined a large corpus of sixth millennium chipped stone artifacts from ᶜAin Ghazal (Abu Ghanimeh 1989) demonstrates that the distinctive PPNC typological and technological constellation (Rollefson 1990) has been overlooked or ignored in surveys in the southern Levant, which have placed PPNC lithic scatters into a fuzzily defined aceramic "PPNB" rubric.

Debitage Classes

Nearly 56,000 chipped stone artifacts were recovered in the 1989 season, tabulated in absolute

Table 1. Absolute Counts and Relative Frequencies for Debitage Classes in
the 1989 Chipped Stone Artifact Samples from ᶜAin Ghazal*

| | | | | | | *Absolute Counts(n)* | | | | | | |
	BL	bl	FL	CTE	BS	MF	DE	OT	PL	COR	(TL)	Totals
M	2314	562	5669	137	181	2472	1171	29	5	162	(1332)	12,702
Y	3510	813	7828	229	353	2644	1873	36	3	142	(1372)	17,431
C	2756	728	6983	179	172	3578	2365	44	2	130	(746)	16,937
LBC	461	104	886	39	23	413	333	9	–	20	(137)	2288
LB	957	177	2786	103	60	1434	1020	19	–	28	(313)	6584
Total											(3984)	55,942
						Relative Frequencies						
	BL	bl	FL	CTE	BS	MF	DE	OT	PL	COR	(TL)	Totals
M	18.3	4.2	46.1	1.1	1.3	19.1	8.3	0.3	0.0	1.4	(10.8)	100.1
Y	20.1	4.8	45.2	1.3	1.9	15.2	10.7	0.2	0.0	0.9	(7.9)	100.3
C	15.1	4.3	40.5	1.0	1.0	22.2	14.9	0.2	0.0	0.8	(4.4)	100.0
LBC	20.4	4.7	38.9	1.8	1.0	17.7	14.2	0.4	0.0	0.9	(6.0)	100.0
LB	14.3	2.9	42.2	1.5	0.9	21.9	15.4	0.2	0.0	0.4	(4.8)	100.1

*Column codes: BL = blades; bl = bladelets; FL = flakes; CTE = core trimming elements; BS = burin spalls; MF = microflakes; DE = debris; OT = "other flakes"; PL = palaeolithic; COR = cores; (TL) = tools (not counted in totals).

Row codes: M = surface and mixed contexts; Y = Yarmoukian; C = PPNC; LBC = Late PPNB/PPNC; LB = Late PPNB. The same codes are used in all of the tables.

counts and relative frequencies according to debitage class in Table 1. The season total is relatively low, especially compared to the amount obtained in 1988, when the area and volume of sediments was smaller.

One reason for the reduced numbers in the 1989 season was the need to use a sampling strategy for sieving excavated deposits because of the time pressures to investigate so large an area. In the South Field, for example, only 25 percent of the soil was sieved in Squares 4453–4654, since an adequate lithic sample was obtained from that area in 1984 and 1988. In Square 6260, the uphill test trench in the South Field, a similar strategy was employed for the Yarmoukian layers, although there half of sediment from the aceramic layers was sieved. Nearly all of the soil in the Central and North Fields was sieved; field notes indicated which layers were totally or partially sieved.

The figures in Table 1 are not strictly comparable, then, with those from earlier seasons, since measures have not yet been taken to account for the sieved vs. unsieved samples. One might expect, for example, that the classes of smaller debitage (such as burin spalls, microflakes, and debris) would be underrepresented since they are more easily missed in the digging process itself, espe-

cially in the Yarmoukian and PPNC layers in the South Field. Comparing Table 1 with the results of the 1988 season (Rollefson, Kafafi, and Simmons 1990: Table 1), this may hold true for the burin spalls, but the relative frequencies for microflakes and debris in 1989 are actually higher in 1989 than in 1988.

Nevertheless, the general trends of the major debitage classes in 1989 match patterns seen in earlier seasons at ᶜAin Ghazal, with one principal exception. The blade-to-flake ratios (Table 2) for the PPNC and Yarmoukian layers parallel the 1984, 1985, and 1988 results (Rollefson and Simmons 1986; 1987; Rollefson, Kafafi, and Simmons 1990), although the Yarmoukian tool percentage in 1989 is relatively high compared to earlier seasons.

The exception to previous patterns is seen in the relative frequencies of debitage classes for the LPPNB deposits, particularly noticeable in the blade-to-flake ratio. Throughout the campaign at ᶜAin Ghazal, the lowest blade-to-flake ratio has consistently been among the PPNC samples, with slightly higher proportions of blades in the Yarmoukian period, and roughly equal numbers of blades and flakes in the PPNB period (both MPPNB and LPPNB). The LPPNB 26:74 ratio for the 1989 season, then, is something of an anomaly,

Table 2. Absolute Counts and Relative Frequencies of Blades and Flakes
from *in situ* Samples from the 1989 Season at ᶜAin Ghazal

	Number				*Percent*		
	Blades	*Flakes*	*Totals*		*Blades*	*Flakes*	*Totals*
Y	3510	7828	11,338		31.0	69.0	100.0
C	2756	6983	9739		28.3	71.7	100.0
LBC	461	886	1347		34.2	65.8	100.0
LB	957	2786	3743		25.6	74.4	100.0

Chi-Square Matrix

	Y	*C*	*LBC*	*LB*
Y	–	17.734	5.973	39.218
C	.001	–	20.172	10.104
LBC	.02	.001	–	36.932
LB	.0001	.01	.0001	–

although it is easily explained by at least two "chipping floors" producing much higher flake counts than normal (e.g., Rollefson and Simmons 1987: 96). Once those samples have been removed from the "non-chipping floor" loci, we expect the blade-to-flake ratio for the LPPNB to approximate the general pattern established in earlier analyses.

Some deposits in the 1989 seasons could not be assigned confidently to either the PPNC or the LPPNB (especially in Squares 3300 and 6891; see above) because of the restricted size of the samples. The figures in Table 2 emphasize the ambiguity, for the 1:2 ratio for blades to flakes for the "LBC" loci falls roughly halfway between the 1:1 PPNB value and the 1:3 ratio for the PPNC.

Tool Typology

Tables 3 and 4 present absolute counts and relative frequencies for the tools recovered in 1989. Once again, earlier patterns are generally maintained, with the burin class dominating all other tool classes in all periods. Earlier reports (e.g., Rollefson, Kafafi, and Simmons 1990; Rollefson 1988) have emphasized the seriational potential of burins, and a reexamination of those tools according to a new burin typology has strengthened that potential. Details of this new approach are being refined; but the preliminary results reveal a marked change in the relative importance of transverse, dihedral, and truncation burins in each of the MPPNB, LPPNB, PPNC and Yarmoukian periods at ᶜAin Ghazal (Rollefson, in press).

The projectile points from 1989 reflect a pattern of larger, heavier "spear points" in the LPPNB (and MPPNB from earlier seasons) as opposed to a greater reliance on smaller "arrowheads" in the PPNC and Yarmoukian periods. In addition to shorter and lighter points in the later periods, there is also an apparent intensification of retouch through the MPPNB-LPPNB-PPNC-Yarmoukian sequence, ranging from a principal focus on marginal retouch in the earlier phases to increasing invasive unifacial retouch (especially on the exterior surface) in the PPNC to a greater reliance on complete bifacial retouch in the Yarmoukian period (J. Eighmey, personal communication).

Knives played a particularly important role in the LPPNB tool inventory, a phenomenon also observed in the 1988 season. Knives are quite variable, and several criteria are used in identifying them. Tabular knives are distinctive and come mostly from the PPNC and Yarmoukian periods, although they are also present in smaller numbers in the LPPNB. Bifacial foliate knives are also frequent in the LPPNB, PPNC, and Yarmoukian periods, but they seem to be absent in MPPNB layers at ᶜAin Ghazal. Some knives bear very delicate microdenticulation throughout the entire cultural sequence, usually exhibiting a distinctive "frosting" that extends a few millimeters from the knife edge toward the center of the tool. In addition to that feature, which is easily visible on casual observation, there is also edge damage barely visible to the naked eye on a large number of pieces, usually blades, which low magnification (20–40 x)

Table 3. Absolute Counts of Chipped Stone Tools from the 1989 Season at ᶜAin Ghazal

Tool Class	Number			
	Y	C	LBC	LB
Spear points	16	8	2	10
Arrowheads	34	21	1	2
Sickles	24	9	4	17
Burins (all types)	284	117	28	45
Truncations	36	19	5	4
Scrapers (all types)	79	31	7	16
Denticulates	101	79	10	14
Notches	101	84	15	21
Perforators	36	22	1	1
Awls/borers	74	24	5	13
Drills	17	5	1	2
Bifaces	5	1	4	4
Axes/adzes/celts	2	8	3	3
Picks	1	3	–	–
Chisels	1	1	–	–
Choppers	6	1	–	1
Wedges	29	9	3	11
Knives	71	48	8	34
Backed blades/flakes	22	5	–	3
Tanged blades	7	5	2	1
Other	9	5	–	3
Subtotal	960	505	99	215
Retouched blades	70	49	9	7
Retouched flakes	87	51	3	10
Utilized blades	83	47	13	24
Utilized flakes	79	50	7	16
Indeterminate	98	44	7	41
Total	1377	746	138	313

Table 4. Relative Frequencies of Major Tool Classes from the 1989 Season at ᶜAin Ghazal

Tool Class	Y	C	LBC	LB
Spear points	1.7	1.6	2.0	4.9
Arrowheads	3.6	4.2	1.0	1.0
Sickles	2.5	1.8	4.0	8.3
Burins	29.7	23.2	28.3	22.0
Truncations	3.8	3.8	5.1	2.0
Scrapers	8.3	6.1	7.1	7.8
Denticulates	10.6	15.6	10.1	6.8
Notches	10.6	16.6	15.2	10.2
Perforators	3.8	4.4	1.0	0.5
Awl/borers	7.7	4.8	5.1	6.3
Drills	1.8	1.0	1.0	1.0
Bifaces	0.5	0.2	4.0	2.0
Axes/adzes	0.2	1.6	3.0	1.5
Picks	0.1	0.6	–	–
Chisels	0.1	0.2	–	–
Choppers	0.6	0.2	–	0.5
Wedges	3.0	1.8	3.0	5.4
Knives	7.4	9.5	8.1	16.6
Backed blades/flakes	2.3	1.0	–	1.5
Tanged blades	0.7	1.0	2.0	0.5
Other	0.9	1.0	–	1.5
Subtotal	99.9	100.2	100.0	100.3
Retouched blades	(5.1)	(6.6)	(6.5)	(2.3)
Retouched flakes	(6.3)	(6.8)	(8.2)	(3.3)
Utilized blades	(6.0)	(6.3)	(9.4)	(7.9)
Utilized flakes	(5.8)	(6.7)	(5.1)	(5.3)
Indeterminate	(7.1)	(5.9)	(5.1)	(13.5)

shows to be clear rounding and polish of the cutting edge.[7]

HUMAN BURIALS[8]

The remains of 23 discernible individual interments were found in 1989 in addition to numerous scattered fragments of human bone. One adolescent from a probable LPPNB context was recovered from a bulldozer section in the Central Field; the arrangement of the bones shows that it was a secondary burial. Two or three other partially preserved burials may be assigned to the LPPNB, but more definite dating must await C-14 assays. The remaining burials all can be assigned confidently to the PPNC, and in all interpretable circum-

stances, they appear to be secondary interments. Notably, skulls are intact with PPNC burials, a departure from MPPNB and LPPNB norms, although the isolated PPNC robust male skull found on the floor of one of the chambers of the house in Square 4655 of the South Field raises some question about this.

The sex-age determinations for all 23 individuals include eight infants (< 12 months), five children (1–12.5 years), one adolescent (12.5–18 years), five adult females (> 18 years), and four adult males. Infant mortality was high, and altogether subadults accounted for well over half of the sample, paralleling results from earlier seasons at ᶜAin Ghazal (Rolston in Rollefson *et al.* 1985).

Pathologies were generally restricted to arthritic degeneration, especially in the feet, a pattern common throughout the samples of the previous five seasons at ᶜAin Ghazal. Dental health was rela-

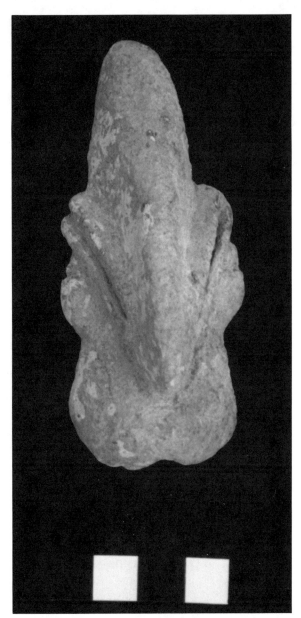

Fig. 11. Front view of the clay Yarmoukian "coffee bean" fertility figurine from ᶜAin Ghazal. Scale: white squares are 1 cm long (photograph by L. Rolston).

Table 5. Bone Tools from the 1989 Season at ᶜAin Ghazal

Type of Bone Tool	Y	C	LBC	LB
Awls	13	27	3	10
Spatulas	1	2	–	5
Needles	4	3	–	3
Polished rib fragments	4	10 [a]	–	–
Polished bone fragments	2	8	3	2
Serrated Bone	–	1 [b]	–	–
Other	1 [c]	–	–	1 [d]

[a] one a "flenser"?
[b] bone "rasp"
[c] "wand"
[d] "polisher"

Table 6. Human and Animal Figurines from the 1989 Season at ᶜAin Ghazal

Type of Figurine	Y	C	LB
Human	3	1	–
Human?	1 [a]	1	–
Goat?	1	–	–
Cow	1	–	1
Animal, indet.	–	1	–
Animal?	–	–	1
Animal horn	1	1	–

Note: All the figurines are of baked or sun-dried clay except: the human?, ([a]) which is of limestone.

tively good, although alveolar resorption (from gum disease) increased with age to sometimes severe proportions. Enamel displasia among adults was common, indicating major health stresses during childhood.

No burials from any of the seasons at ᶜAin Ghazal can be ascribed to the Yarmoukian period, although one relatively intact interment from the Central Field falls into the Aceramic/Ceramic transitional phase. It is admittedly speculative at this point, but it appears possible that the Yarmoukian populations at ᶜAin Ghazal chose to bury their dead outside the village proper, signaling a major change in social ritual for the first time in the Neolithic.

FAUNAL REMAINS[9]

Animal bones again were abundantly produced in the 1989 season, far outnumbering all other artifacts combined. Thick calcareous encrustations on Yarmoukian and PPNC samples continue to hamper identifications, and the sheer volume has slowed meaningful interpretations so soon after the close of the season.

Few remarks can be made at this stage of the analysis, although the general patterns witnessed

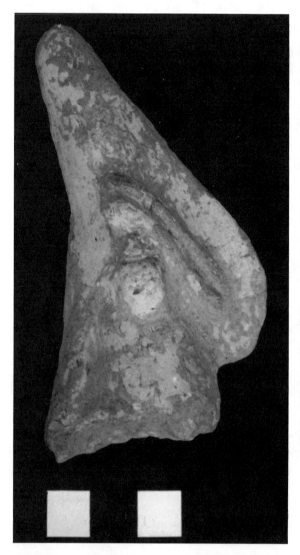

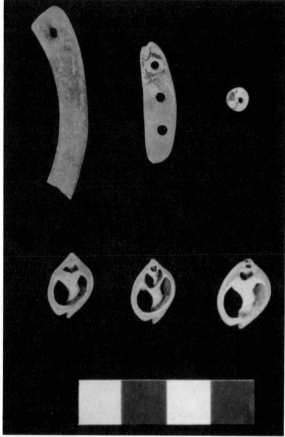

Fig. 13. Mother-of-pearl pendant (top left) and "button" (top right), both PPNC; bone pendant (top center) and shell beads (bottom), all LPPNB. Scale: white squares are 1 cm long (photograph by L. Rolston).

Fig. 12. Right profile of the figurine in fig. 11. Note the bulge just below the eye, perhaps representing an earring (photograph by L. Rolston).

OTHER FINDS

Bone Tools

Table 5 presents the counts of the bone tools identified so far from the 1989 season, but many more examples will be produced as the faunal analysis proceeds. Overall, there is little difference indicated in Table 5 from samples recovered in earlier seasons.

Figurines

Only 13 figurines, all but one made of clay, were recovered in the 1989 season (Table 6). The scarcity of figurines from LPPNB contexts probably reflects the restricted area and volume of excavated sediments attributable to this period. The poor state of preservation of both the animal and

in earlier years have been maintained. The number of vertebrate species assignable to the PPNC and Yarmoukian periods has increased somewhat from earlier counts (cf. Köhler-Rollefson, Gillespie, and Metzger 1988), but the decrease in the number of species in those periods from that of the MPPNB continues to be dramatic. The decline in species variety appears to have begun during the LPPNB, indicating a rapidly degraded environment and loss of habitat variety sometime in the latter half of the seventh millennium (cf. Köhler-Rollefson and Rollefson 1990). Rate of habitat depletion must await the results of radiocarbon dating.

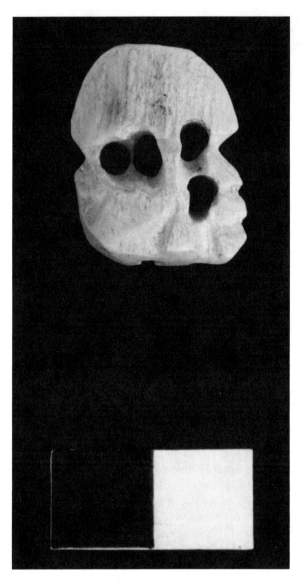

Fig. 14. Anthropomorphic pendant of hippopotamus tusk ivory. Scale: white square is 1 cm long (photograph by L. Rolston).

Table 7. Ornaments from the 1989 Season at ᶜAin Ghazal

Ornament	Y	C	LBC	LB
Bracelets				
Limestone	28	40 [a]	2	5
Alabaster(?)	1	2	–	1
Basalt	–	–	1	–
Beads				
Limestone	–	1	–	–
Snail shell	–	1	–	5
Greenstone	–	1	–	–
Turquoise	–	1	–	–
Pendants				
Mother-of-pearl	1	7 [b]	–	–
Cowrie	4	–	1	1
Sweet clam	2	1	–	1 [c]
Ivory	2	–	–	–
Boar tusk	–	1	–	–
Carnivore teeth	3	–	–	–
Bone	–	–	–	1 [d]
Limestone	–	1	–	–
"Blackstone"	–	1	–	–
Finger (?) rings				
Limestone	–	2	–	1
Bone	2	2	–	1
Button, mother-of-pearl	–	1 [e]	–	–
Carnelian chunk	1	–	–	–
Greenstone chunk	–	1	–	–

[a] one is perforated
[b] two are double perforated
[c] incised?
[d] triple perforated
[e] double perforated

the two human figurines from the PPNC severely limits any interpretation. The same holds for the Yarmoukian specimens, although three are splendid human depictions, including a lovely "coffee bean" example (cf. Perrot 1966: pls. 6–13, 16–17), an incised limestone pebble (cf. Stekelis 1950: pls. 3–5), and an as yet unique "parted-hair" head (figs. 11, 12). Among the animal figurines, one probable goat came from a Yarmoukian context, the first example of that animal for this period. (See below for the description of an ivory pendant in the form of a human head).

Ornaments

Table 7 tabulates the small finds associated with ornamentation; "bracelets," common in the LPPNB, PPNC, and Yarmoukian deposits, dominate the collection as they did in earlier seasons. Beads were not numerous, perhaps reflecting to some degree the reduced sieving in 1989. It is not known yet if the greenstone bead from the PPNC is made of copper ore or of "Dhabba marble," although the former is more likely. Five beads/pendants made of ground snail shell came from the LPPNB building in Square 5518 (fig. 13). Of particular note is a lovely anthropomorphic pendant made of hippopotamus tusk ivory (fig. 14) from the Yarmoukian period. Although hippopotamus lived along the Levantine coast throughout the Late Pleistocene and

Fig. 15. PPNC *mancala* game board, made of limestone. Scale: white rectangles are 5 cm long (photograph by L. Rolston).

Table 8. Miscellaneous Objects from *in situ* Deposits of the 1989 Season at ᶜAin Ghazal

Object	Y	C	LB
Game board, limestone	–	1	–
Painted bone fragment	–	–	1 [a]
Obsidian chips	1	8	–
Geometric objects			
Sphere, limestone	–	1	1
Sphere, plaster/chalk	–	1	–
Macehead, basalt	1	–	–
Stone "cup", limestone	1	–	–
Perforated stone weights	4	1	–
Whorls, limestone	–	3	–
Double-perforated stone object	1	–	–
Pointed rod, limestone	–	1	–
Incised limestone object	1	–	–
"Worked" limestone piece	1	2	–
Plaster "nail"	1	–	–
Plaster cylinder	1	1	–
Shaped plaster/chalk fragment	1	–	1
Cord-impressed plaster piece	–	1	–
Pottery disc	1	–	–
Shaped clay (burned)	–	–	1

[a] turquoise pigment

well into the Holocene periods (Uerpmann 1987: 46), this is the first known example of such material being used for jewelry or human representation (or any other artifact, for that matter) in the Levantine Neolithic.

Miscellaneous Objects[10]

Artifacts that do not fit the categories described so far are listed in Table 8. Most of them require little comment, although three categories deserve some discussion.

The obsidian chips from the 1989 season were principally from PPNC contexts, although a single fragment was found in a Yarmoukian locus. They bring the total of that exotic resource from all of the excavation seasons to almost 40 pieces. There appears to be a shift in the source of obsidian during the occupation of ᶜAin Ghazal. The obsidian from the MPPNB layers is invariably a dense black, while the PPNC and Yarmoukian examples are usually a smoky gray, suggesting some change in the exchange pattern with the eastern parts of Anatolia.

The "painted bone" fragment from a LPPNB locus in Square 5518 is the first example of painted bone found at ᶜAin Ghazal. It is only a fragment, so what the original artifact was cannot be determined. Turquoise-colored pigment on the piece, however, suggests some parallel with painted bone figurines of a ritual nature from the Nahal Hemar cave (Bar-Yosef and Alon 1988: 21–23).

Finally, one artifact of "miscellaneous" character adds some measure of serendipity to the PPNC inhabitants of ᶜAin Ghazal, for a slab of pecked and incised limestone indicates that the people enjoyed game-playing, something that was already widespread in Jordan during the Neolithic (Rollefson 1992). The pattern of cup-marks on the sub-rectangular and thin slab (fig. 15), found in the fill of the southernmost PPNC house in the South Field, is still seen in *mancala* games played throughout the modern Arab world and across most of Africa. The people of ᶜAin Ghazal may have begun to feel the effects of a deteriorating environment, but they still had the time to relieve their anxiety by engaging in vigorous competitions of mental skill.

CONCLUDING REMARKS

The 1989 season at ᶜAin Ghazal will be the last excavation at this wonderful settlement until the problems associated with the commercial and residential developments planned by the Municipality of ᶜAmman are finally sorted out. Signed agreements provide that at least ten percent of the site, the "core area," will be preserved as an open-air museum available for both public education and future archaeological investigation, but the inevitable problems of loop-holes and enforcement of local antiquities laws remain. Negotiations with the United States Agency for International Development for funds to preserve the ten percent area are still underway, but it cannot be projected what the chances of success for realizing the open-air museum are at present.

Despite this pessimistic view, there still remains an enormous amount of analysis to be conducted on the materials from the past six seasons of excavation at ᶜAin Ghazal. Arrangements are being made to publish the final site report.

NOTES

[1] The excavations at ᶜAin Ghazal are a joint project of San Diego State University, Yarmouk University, and the Desert Research Institute of the University of Nevada system. In addition to support from those institutions, major funding was provided by the National Geographic Society (Grant No. 4069-89); the National Endowment for the Humanities (Grant No. RO-21633-88); AMOCO Corporation; ALIA, the Royal Jordanian Airline; the Cobb Institute of Archaeology, Mississippi State University; and EARTHWATCH. We also thank the Department of Antiquities of Jordan for facilitating the work, and M. Ibrahim, K. Abu Ghanimeh, and ACOR Director B. De Vries for their invaluable assistance.

[2] A stratified sample of this three-floor sequence is now being analyzed by P. Vandiver of the Smithsonian Institution.

[3] The three dates assigned to Levels II–III at Beidha come from a single charcoal sample (Weinstein 1984). All three dates (assayed at different laboratories) are relatively dispersed, and there are contradictions with the general sequence of dates from other occupational episodes at the site. Despite the absence of any apparent stratigraphic interruption at Beidha (B. Byrd, personal communication), it is possible that a PPNC episode occurred there that reused Late PPNB structures, as suggested by the evidence at ᶜAin Ghazal. Ten radiocarbon samples from PPNC deposits at ᶜAin Ghazal are currently being processed at the University of Arizona (as well as two Yarmoukian samples), and additional radiocarbon samples are to be assayed from Beidha (B. Byrd, personal communication). The results in the near future should resolve the issue.

[4] Several extensive terrace walls that step up the slope, each extending for well over 200 m in the North Field, are made of "field stones," including several examples of large querns. It is quite apparent that most of the "field stones" are the remains of destroyed Neolithic structures that were bulldozed within the past three or four decades.

[5] The rich flotation samples have been sent to R. Neef, Groningen University, for analysis and dating.

[6] We owe a debt of gratitude to D. Olszewski for conducting the preliminary debitage sorting and much of the typological classification of tools for the 1984, 1988, and 1989 seasons.

[7] Knives in the 1982–1985 samples are probably seriously underrepresented, especially for the MPPNB, because of the admittedly rapid typing system. It is likely that many of the "utilized" blades and flakes may be assigned to the knife category, and a considerable effort to reanalyze these samples is called for.

[8] The following brief synopsis is based on the work of S. Rolston, the project's Senior Human Osteologist, and the dedicated work of C. Butler, Assistant Human Osteologist.

[9] I. Köhler-Rollefson and L. Quintero are the Senior Faunal Analysts for the ᶜAin Ghazal Project, and we acknowledge their devotion to the analysis of the enormous corpus of faunal remains.

[10] Results of the analysis of groundstone objects from the 1989 season are not yet available.

BIBLIOGRAPHY

Abu Ghanimeh, Kh.
1989   *Le Néolithique précéramique en Jordanie: étude de l'industrie lithique du secteur sud d'Ain Ghazal.* Unpublished doctoral dissertation, Université de Bordeaux.

Bar-Yosef, O., and Alon, D.
1988   Nahal Hemar Cave. *ᶜAtiqot* 18.

Kirkbride, D.
1966   Five Seasons at the Pre-Pottery Neolithic Village of Beidha in Jordan. *Palestine Exploration Quarterly* 98: 8–72.

Köhler-Rollefson, I.; Gillespie, W.; and Metzger, M.
1988   The Fauna from Neolithic ᶜAin Ghazal. Pp. 423–30 in *The Prehistory of Jordan*, eds. A. Garrard and H. Gebel. BAR International Series 396. Oxford: British Archaeological Reports.

Köhler-Rollefson, I., and Rollefson, G.
1990   The Impact of Neolithic Subsistence Strategies on the Environment: The Case of ᶜAin Ghazal, Jordan. Pp. 3–14 in S. Bottema, G. Entjes-Nieborg and W. van Zeist, eds., *Man's Role in the Shaping of the Eastern Mediterranean Landscape.* Rotterdam: Balkema.

Nissen, H.; Muheisen, M.; Gebel, H.; Becker, C.; Neef, R.; Pachur, H.; Qadi, N.; and Schultz, M.
1987   Report on the First Two Seasons of Excavation at Basta (1986–1987). *Annual of the Department of Antiquities of Jordan* 31: 79–119.

Perrot, J.
1966   La troisième campagnes de fouilles à Munhata (1964). *Syria* 43: 49–63.

Rollefson, G.
1988   Stratified Burin Classes at ᶜAin Ghazal: Implications for the Desert Neolithic of Jordan. Pp. 437–49 in *The Prehistory of Jordan*, eds. A. Garrard and H. Gebel. BAR International Series 396. Oxford: British Archaeological Reports.
1990   Neolithic Chipped Stone Technology at ᶜAin Ghazal: The Status of the PPNC. *Paleorient* 16(1): 119–24.
1992   A Neolithic Game Board from ᶜAin Ghazal, Jordan. *Bulletin of the American Schools of Oriental Research* 286: 1–5.

In press   The PPNC Phase of the Aceramic Neolithic of the Southern Levant. Paper presented to the Third Symposium on Upper Paleolithic, Mesolithic, and Neolithic Populations of Europe and the Mediterranean Basin, Budapest, September, 1990.

Rollefson, G.; Kafafi, Z.; and Simmons, A.
1990   The Neolithic Village of ᶜAin Ghazal, Jordan: Preliminary Report on the 1988 Season. *Bulletin of the American Schools of Oriental Research Supplement* 27: 95–116.

Rollefson, G., and Simmons, A.
1985   The Early Neolithic Village of ᶜAin Ghazal, Jordan: Preliminary Report on the 1983 Season. *Bulletin of the American Schools of Oriental Research Supplement* 23: 35–52.
1986   The Neolithic Village of ᶜAin Ghazal, Jordan: Preliminary Report on the 1984 Season. *Bulletin of the American Schools of Oriental Research Supplement* 24: 147–64.
1987   The Neolithic Village of ᶜAin Ghazal, Jordan: Preliminary Report on the 1985 Season. *Bulletin of the American Schools of Oriental Research Supplement* 25: 93–106.
1988   The Neolithic Settlement at ᶜAin Ghazal. Pp. 393–421 in *The Prehistory of Jordan*, eds. A. Garrard and H. Gebel. BAR International Series 396. Oxford: British Archaeological Reports.

Rollefson, G.; Simmons, A.; Donaldson, M.; Gillespie, W.; Kafafi, Z.; Köhler-Rollefson, I.; McAdam, E.; and Rolston, S.
1985   Excavation at the Pre-Pottery Neolithic B (PPNB) Village of ᶜAin Ghazal (Jordan), 1983. *Mitteilungen der Deutschen Orient Gesellschaft* 117: 69–116.

Stekelis, M.
1950   A New Neolithic Industry: The Yarmukian of Palestine. *Israel Exploration Journal* 1: 1–19.

Uerpmann, H.
1987   *The Ancient Distribution of Ungulate Mammals in the Middle East.* Beihefte zum Tübinger Atlas des Vorderen Orients, Reihe A (Naturwissenschaften) 27. Wiesbaden: Reichert.

Weinstein, J.
1984   Radiocarbon Dating in the Southern Levant. *Radiocarbon* 26(3): 297–366.